Daring to Heal

Growing Beyond Trauma Through Awareness, Acceptance, & Action

LAURA STEARNS

ISBN: 979-8-9926273-1-2 (Kindle)
ISBN: 979-8-9926273-0-5 (Print)
ISBN: 979-8-9926273-2-9 (eBook)

Book design by Booknook.biz

Dedication

For Tucker and Calvin

Contents

Part One

Transforming Negative Thinking

Chapter One

An Introduction

"Trauma" may seem like one of those overused words, but the truth is we're walking around on a planet with literally billions of people who suffer from some form of trauma. The sources of it are seemingly unlimited: discrimination and harassment; witnessing domestic violence or abuse; experiencing physical, emotional, and sexual violence in our relationships; physical injury whether intended, such as surgery, or accidental, such as a car crash; cultural oppression, and genocide; and participating in policing and military incidents as a receiver of harm or as an enforcer. The list can go on and on.

The reasons for emotional suffering are unique, but there are commonalities in what trauma does to us on the inside as human beings. Parts of us fracture emotionally and psychologically, we become frozen in elements of our development. Our natural ability to process and heal can get interrupted, and the way we participate in our relationships can be greatly affected. We can be fully functioning in most of our daily activities, and sadly incapable in ways that don't seem logical. Trauma defies reason.

Concerns around trauma are surfacing in so many different conversations around the globe. The COVID-19 pandemic caused many of us to slow down and pay close attention to our bodies and mental health, and it also devastated communities, stressed frontline workers, and caused people to lose their jobs. And there's the very real issue of the rise in domestic violence during the shutdown. People have been pushed beyond their limits and then some. Children suffered greatly worldwide from the disruption in their learning processes and social development, and those who live in homes where domestic violence or child abuse is prevalent had little or no escape from it. We'll be seeing the repercussions of this for decades. Trauma is everywhere and this reality feels overwhelming.

I'm not a clinician; I'm a trauma survivor. This book is the companion to my book *Shattered: Exposing the Open Secret of the Children's Theatre Scandal ~ A Memoir of Harm and Healing.* When I set out to write about my life, I knew I didn't want to just reveal the intimate details of what happened to me; I wanted the sharing of it to matter beyond my own need for the truth to be known. This is the outcome of my desire to use my experience and personal healing processes as a tool to help others move forward on their wellness journey, no matter how trauma has shown up in their life. My personal lens is childhood sexual violence, but the tools offered in this book can work for anyone because I'm addressing the human condition of how we're affected by it, not the cause of trauma.

Wounds fester if kept in the dark, they need air and sunshine to support the body's natural healing process. Healing happens in the light. I believe it's the same for wounds of the mind and spirit. For me, the silence I kept around the physical, psychological, and emotional wounds from childhood sexual abuse kept me in the shadows and didn't allow me to heal. There were aspects of me that were arrested in my childhood because of it. It was breaking my silence that started my journey towards deep healing. Those atrophied parts of me have begun to develop as I've healed, my pieces have come together in a way that makes sense and feels right. I still have work to do, but I feel like a whole person now. I'm in my fifties and I finally feel like a grown-up.

For those who took the time to read my memoir, thank you. The gift of witnessing is more valuable than you can imagine. It can give a person permission to remove the shackles of shame attached to abuse, return self-agency, and transform damaging behavioral patterns and self-perceptions. Reading my memoir might provide a deeper level of understanding as you read this book. But as is the case with healthy relationships, this book can easily stand on its own.

I'll have to do a little recap regardless. When watching the next episode of your favorite TV show, you get the "previously on..." section to bring everyone to the same point in the story so you can all move on together. Here's my drastically abridged version.

I grew up in a white middle-class family in Minneapolis, Minnesota in the 1970s and 80s. After being raped by a teenage boy in my own bedroom at the age of ten, a false belief solidified in my mind—*I don't have much say in what happens to my body*. Because he threatened to do it again if I told anyone, I didn't speak of it for many years. This kept me emotionally paralyzed in key parts of my life for decades.

Because the nature of sexual violence often primes the victim to be vulnerable for more of the same, I was raped three more times before I turned twenty. The second time was at the age of fifteen, at a private conservatory for theater performance and production, by an adult actor/teacher at the school. This conservatory was attached to a professional theater called The Children's Theatre Company (CTC) which was run by a man named John Clark Donahue, who had a reputation as a difficult genius.

He was also a pedophile.

The environment he created at CTC was a safe haven for sexual predators, where the sexualization of children was normalized, the barriers between children and adults were removed, and a philosophy of otherness was instilled in the students. Humiliation and cruel humor were used as tools for teaching and getting artists to attain perfection.

This was my high school.

Donahue was arrested on seven counts of criminal sexual conduct with male students in 1984. CTC survived the scandal, in part because the full truth of what was happening there took decades to uncover. The school, however, shut down in 1986, the year after I graduated high school.

In May 2013, The Minnesota Child Victims Act became law, giving victim-survivors a legal platform to speak the truth about what happened to them as children. A three-year retroactive window was created for victims to come forward with cases that happened prior to the establishment of the law. On December 1, 2015, I filed a civil lawsuit, breaking my thirty-plus-year silence about what happened to me as a child, and in the months that followed sixteen more cases were brought forward. Through the investigation for my trial, which occurred in January of 2019, twenty-eight adult perpetrators were identified. The scope of harm done to the children at CTC is vast and varied, and even though only a few civil cases were filed it could have been much more.

Breaking my silence was life-changing in profoundly healing ways, but it had a huge emotional cost too. My legal battle lasted more than four years, and I spent most of that time swimming around in the trauma pool—better known as our legal system. While I was dealing with hidden and unresolved complex trauma, at the same time I was trying to navigate a relentlessly re-traumatizing litigation process and legal system that doesn't understand trauma-informed care.

Over the course of decades, with the accompaniment of skilled practitioners, facilitators, fellow survivors, and a variety of written sources, I've learned ways to help mitigate the effects of my trauma. Through that personal investigation, I've learned a few things, not just about myself but about how trauma affects the brain, and how social systems contribute to a culture of complicity around trauma. I'll share some tools in this book that I hope will be useful and accessible, helping you see a path of your own by showing you mine. Some of these concepts and ideas have been around for centuries, but I will try to explain them with a fresh perspective that makes sense to you.

One such tool is the 3 A's: Awareness, Acceptance, and Action. This is a powerful lens to look through when investigating how we participate in our own lives. There's groundwork that must be laid to understand the depth of these seemingly simple words, and it won't always be easy to absorb.

I'll share a couple of journaling tools I call Identifying False Core Beliefs and The RITE Thinking Process, which I developed over two decades, that help me see the truth about the stories I tell myself. These writing exercises can help shift negative thinking patterns regardless of what's at the heart of the thoughts.

As I was writing about the ways I've gone about transforming my harmful thinking through the lens of the 3 A's, it occurred to me that this tool could easily be applied to larger conversations. As an advocate for healing, I want to help move us all away from the traps of Rape Culture and toward the power of a Culture of Consent. I decided to look at this cultural blemish more closely through this lens.

Consider this book a tool for transforming ourselves and the world around us. You can certainly use its contents like an "a la carte menu," but I believe there's information in each of the sections that are useful to all, and the content can easily translate to a variety of scenarios. The effects of trauma are universal. Harmful social structures like Rape Culture are built on common social contracts and constructs that uphold destructive social norms like racism, sexism, ageism, and all the other "isms" that keep us from being our best selves.

A special note to those in Twelve Step Recovery: Much of what I've learned and incorporated into this book was passed on to me in Twelve Step Recovery. I'm deeply grateful for the wisdom of those who came before me, for the friendships I developed in those rooms, and for a power greater than myself for helping me get out of my own way. Though this is not a book about recovery in those programs, I hope you can use what you learn here as a tool in your journey of self-discovery.

For an individual, you can mine whatever gems you can find for your personal use, or you might have a book club that wants to take that journey together. Teachers might use this in a classroom to help students understand elements of trauma-informed care. Professionals could add it to their arsenal of resources. If you find yourself in the middle of an apocalypse you could use it as kindling...on the other hand, don't—if you're in that kind of social upheaval you might need these tools to keep you grounded. Tuck it into your backpack next to your first aid supplies and energy bars.

I'm going to pose questions at the end of some sections, things for you to ponder and let roll around in your mind to see what comes up. Thoughts you might choose to sit with and wonder about before you move on. Or not. Take them or leave them. You have full agency in this journey of personal investigation.

It's important to take care of yourself as you read this book, and self-care can be hard. Somewhere along the way I got attached to the notion that self-care was sel-*fish*, so I put personal well-being at the end of my list—sometimes I wasn't even on the list. If I did prioritize myself, it was often followed by crushing guilt or shame. If that kind of thinking resonates with you, I encourage you to let it go and allow yourself to indulge in some self-care.

I was never a fan of the term "self-help." I have an aversion to doing things that are trendy. My first instinct when I hear about fad diets and books that promise to make you richer, more productive, or enlightened, is to roll my eyes. I understand now that self-care is a gift we can give ourselves, and that we deserve to be happy and healthy, so I'm letting go of my judgment of the term "self-help" and hope you will, too, if you're feeling the urge to eye roll. I'm not promising you anything here—I'm inviting you to an investigation. The concepts and exercises found within can help create a shift in yourself and the world around you.

I've yet to find a one-size-fits-all remedy for emotional or spiritual healing. Wouldn't it be nice if there were? In my experience, I've needed to look at how I participate in the living of my life from multiple angles, using a variety of tools to see what's what. All of these practices have helped me understand myself better and identify the root of my issues so I can make more informed choices.

My understanding of the concepts I share in this book has grown over time. I encourage you to take notes as you read. I have one book in my arsenal that I've read a dozen times, underlining or highlighting sections that resonate with me and making notes in the margins. Each time I read it I find something different because of who I am in that moment, and my ability to process and absorb the contents evolves as I evolve. Then I add more notes—I like seeing how my understanding has grown over time in the margins. Unless you've borrowed this book, feel free to mark it up in whatever way works for you.

There are a few things I'd like you to think about in order to practice self-care as you read:

- Self-compassion: Be kind to yourself. If something you read causes you to think negatively about yourself, give yourself the same kindness you'd give to a friend who's struggling.
- Be Patient: If something doesn't make sense right away, sit with it. There are concepts in this book that took me years to understand—some of them will need time to germinate for a while before they are fruitful for you.
- Take Your Time: Rushing through isn't going to help you accomplish the goals in this book. If you feel like you need to stop and take a break, do it. If difficult emotions come up, stop and tend to them.

A few words for trauma survivors: If you find yourself unable to concentrate, feel disconnected, or emotionally overwhelmed while reading this book, it's likely that your sympathetic nervous system has fired up, meaning the part of your brain that senses danger is on alert. Breathe deeply. Try to stay in the moment. Going for a walk can help immensely because it engages both sides of the body and brain, which can re-boot your prefrontal cortex, bringing your logical brain back online. This can mitigate the effects of feeling dysregulated. If walking isn't an option, even shifting your eyes from side to side can help. Above all, please take care of yourself while you absorb the contents of this book. It is possible to get through whatever it is you're going through. Breathe. You got this.

I offer you my hand now, as we walk forward. I'll pick up a magnifying glass and we can look at this stuff up close, together. Here we go!

Chapter Two

The Foundation

In December of 2022, I was on the verge of a mental breakdown. I'd stepped away from my work in theater, largely because it was too hard to keep from getting triggered every time I went to work or saw a show. Save for a few theaters that felt good to be in, my experience with the litigation against The Children's Theatre Company had taken its toll on me, and theater in general no longer felt safe or healthy.

I was working at the Sexual Violence Center in Minneapolis, doing work I felt was important and meaningful; helping survivors is gratifying. It was also keeping me so close to my own trauma, that I was having a hard time staying regulated and was terribly depressed. It was an exceptionally cold and dismal December. I suffer from Seasonal Affect Disorder and was using light therapy boxes at work and home, which helped but certainly weren't enough to lift me out of my depression. I'd filled the west-facing window of my apartment with plants earlier in the year, trying something new to keep my spirits up during the grey winter months.

As I lay awake one night, unable to sleep, something deep inside me, down in my belly, spoke. "It's time to go," it said. Go? Go where? I didn't want to listen, but this "voice" is something I've learned to trust. Call it what you will: intuition, The Universe, God— however you define it, it's powerful. When it speaks to me, I can't ignore it for long. I knew it was coming from something other than my own thinking because it gave me pause and scared me a little. When that happens, I know The Universe is talking, not my ego. Something— not my thinking— is guiding me.

A few days later I was talking to my therapist about the struggles

I was having at my job. I felt like I was doing good work and was building a network of friends in the advocacy field. I had originally thought I'd work there for a year and then assess my options. I was only six months into my self-imposed commitment at that point, but I was so depressed. I considered out loud with her the possibility of moving on, giving my notice in a few months, and staying to make sure my replacement was up to speed before leaving. "What if you just gave your notice now and didn't worry about who would replace you?" she asked. That wasn't what I wanted to hear. I didn't want to give up. I'm a caretaker, I don't want to let anyone down. And yet, I could feel in my belly that she was right. I told her I'd think about it.

The next day I had a conversation with a dear friend who listened to all of my woes. I told her that I was having this feeling that I needed to do something drastic. I'd spent two months in California the previous winter, escaping the bitter cold, and considered at that time what it would be like to live there year-round—I wasn't sure I could take another Minnesota winter. But here I was, heading into another one, having suicidal ideation before we'd even gotten to the worst of it; January and February are typically the coldest months with the least amount of sunlight. I told her about my fears of what the coming months might do to me mentally. She said, "I love you, and I don't really want you to move, but what's stopping you from leaving?" I thought about it. "Nothing," I said. I'd changed my lease the past summer to a month-to-month agreement. Again, that little voice inside me said, "It's time to go." Louder this time. I couldn't deny it. It was then I realized "it's time to go" didn't just mean my job. It meant Minnesota. I decided it was time to listen to that belly voice and design the life I wanted to live.

That conversation happened on a Saturday. By Monday, I'd given notice to my landlord and found myself sitting in my boss's office telling her I was leaving. She totally understood my reasons and believed it was the best choice for my mental health. I told her I was considering moving to California. "What will you do," she asked. "I really don't know," I confessed. We discussed possible administrative options in the advocacy world that might be a good fit. But there was that voice again. "Time to advocate for yourself," it was saying. I told her I'd let her know if I needed a reference and thanked her. I was pretty sure I wouldn't continue in the direction of rape crisis advocacy. I was desperately missing my theater work— an artist not making art is a wretched thing, and I was truly pining for something creative to do. If anything, I would pursue my work as an Intimacy Director for theater, film, and TV. If I wanted to continue to focus on advocacy, it would be in the arts.

Two weeks later, I was saying my goodbyes at work and went about preparing to put my things in storage. I had no clue what I was going to do. All I knew was that I couldn't stay, and I trusted that little voice wasn't going to steer me wrong.

Soon after I was having a conversation with a dear friend in Melbourne, Australia. She was getting ready to direct a show and needed an Assistant Director and Intimacy Coach for her creative team. Within days I was purchasing a ticket to Melbourne to spend a month doing AD and Intimacy duties for theater with one of my best friends in the world. And they were entering their summer months in Australia, so I could leave my Happy Lights behind. My brother was more than happy to take all my plants. Things were starting to fall into place without effort.

I knew I would not want to stay in Minnesota after my trip Down Under, so I reached out to friends in California. Their guest house happened to be sitting empty and they were happy to have me come and stay with them until I figured out what I wanted to do. After a truly joyful experience in Melbourne and a brief time back in Minneapolis, I packed up everything that was a "must have" into my car— including my faithful dog, Wilbur— left the rest in storage and drove west.

The casita behind my friend's home became a sanctuary for healing. The saltwater swimming pool five feet from my door was like baptismal water and I swam and floated in it every day, soaking up the healing energy of the salt and California sun— with sunscreen of course. For the first time in my life, I focused on and attended to my own needs and mine alone. I ate good food, visited with friends, watched movies and binged shows, cried if I needed to, took long walks with Wilbur every day, and read books. And I slept— I didn't know how exhausted I was until I took the time to rest, and not just for a weekend or a week. I did this for three months. It was possibly the single most important gift of my life— the time to heal, do therapy and figure out what I needed to do, and I'm eternally grateful to my friends for making that possible.

I flew back to Minneapolis in the fall of 2023 to direct a show. Being there after months of absorbing the healing energy of California was okay, but it was clear to me that I'd made the right decision to leave— thanks, little voice. When I flew back, I found myself relaxing at the sight of the Sierra Nevada Mountains through the little window of the plane. I was home. I decided it was time to commit and put down roots in Southern California.

I spent my life mired down in trauma, making decisions based on old thinking that was planted in fear. I was deeply wounded as a child and found some relief through Twelve Step work, therapy, and developing the tools I share in this book. But it wasn't until I addressed the thing at the heart of my pain, unresolved trauma, and untreated PTSD, that I was able to finally hear and fully trust that voice.

When I let go and allowed myself to set my fear aside and be guided, things started falling into place. The ease with which I let go of belongings that no longer served me, the opportunity in Melbourne, my friends having a place for me to live in California, I got out of my own way and it all just— happened. The gifts I have been given, the deepened friendships, the satisfying work I'm doing now, the lovely little theater community I've found myself in, my new home that I love beyond belief, none of this would have happened if I hadn't had access to that voice. Clearing away the clutter in my brain with the tools I share in this book, and healing my trauma, gave me access to that voice calling to me from my belly. I would not be living the life am I today, which is pretty wonderful, if I hadn't turned down the volume of the trauma story in my head enough to hear it.

That's what the first part of this book is about— clearing the clutter. I can't heal your trauma for you, or turn up the volume so you can hear your own internal voice. What I can do is offer you some tools to help you clear your clutter, which can give you access to something that can alter your life— truth. Your truth.

~ What is Trauma? ~

I like dictionaries and encyclopedias—I always carried a pocket-size dictionary in my school bag as a kid. When I don't know the meaning of a word, I don't usually ask someone what it means, because then they would see through my façade and figure out that I'm a complete fraud and really not smart at all—this stems from my false belief that I'm stupid. Instead, I go to the dictionary and read through all the definitions of the word until I find the one that brings clarity. I'll refer to the tried-and-true dictionary when I think it may be helpful.

If there's a word or phrase that you don't understand and I don't provide a definition, look it up. When I keep reading after coming across a word I don't know, I often spend a lot of brain energy trying to figure out the meaning when I should be paying attention to the words I'm reading. I end up going back and re-reading chunks of text because my brain was too busy trying to figure out the word from two paragraphs earlier. It's a huge waste of time that I could have used to look up the word in the first place. Give yourself the gift of understanding when you need to. Don't leave a part of your brain behind, hooked on a question like, "What does 'excoriate' even mean?" Look it up! OK, now I'm going to have to define that for those who don't know. I'll provide footnotes at the bottom of the page for quick access when I do.[1]

It's important to have some foundational context for some of the concepts at the heart of this book. Before I dive into the deep end, here's a brief overview of the basic things you need to know[2].

Events can be traumatic, like a house fire, and a body can expe-

---

[1] Excoriate: to criticize (someone or something) very harshly. Merriam-Webster. com

[2] This section is deliberately concise and by no means comprehensive. Volumes could be written about each topic.

rience trauma, such as a broken bone. I'm talking about the unique effects experienced by a person because of a traumatic event or multiple events.

Two people can have the same experience and be affected in completely different ways. For example, everyone I know who watched the Twin Towers collapse on 9/11 was horrified by what they saw, but it had a different impact on the people who knew someone in those buildings.

Trauma is a normal human response to abnormal events. People experience trauma physically, mentally, and emotionally. The type of trauma individuals experience will affect how they respond to it. Trauma is divided into three main types:

- Acute trauma: a single incident.
- Chronic trauma: repeated and prolonged trauma, like domestic violence or abuse.
- Complex trauma: exposure to various and multiple traumatic events over time.

No two trauma stories are identical. Everyone with a traumatic experience has a life story that colors the effects and impact of the trauma event. The effects of trauma can land very differently psychologically and physically in the body for multiple reasons:

- Age.
- The family situation, such as stability or safety in the home.
- Previous emotional trauma, such as a death in the family.
- Former life experiences, such as physical or sexual abuse.
- How the person's brain normally processes information, and their ability to understand what's happening.
- Communication style.
- Mental health issues, such as a predisposition to depression or anxiety.
- The nature of the victim's support system at the time of the event.

The type of trauma also comes into play: acute, chronic, or complex. Comparing experiences is unfair to another person who has suffered some form of trauma. It's also unfair to yourself if you're downgrading your own experience because it doesn't look as bad as that of another victim. The bottom line is that trauma is trauma, and your experience is your own. We need to recognize and appreciate the complexities of each person's trauma story.

Not everyone reacts to similar circumstances the same way. Someone who experienced trauma as a child and then again later in life will have a different reaction to that assault than a victim who is assaulted for the first time as an adult. Someone who grew up in a home where family members yelled at each other all the time is going to react differently to a traumatic experience than a person who was an only child and grew up in a quiet home. Context matters.

How a person sees themselves after they've experienced trauma is nuanced. The terms "victim" and "survivor" can be very personal. There's no one-size-fits-all term. For some, the word "victim" is accurate for them because it speaks to the powerlessness of things beyond their control. Others prefer the term "survivor" because it speaks to who they are now or what they survived.

I don't like to use the term "victim" to describe myself because I don't want to be emotionally stuck in or defined by the event of being victimized. I prefer the term "survivor" because it implies movement. I *was* a victim of a crime, but *now* I'm a survivor. To be inclusive, I'll primarily use the term "victim-survivor" in this book, so everyone feels seen.

~ Trauma and the Brain ~

When a person experiences an overwhelming event that's out of their control, the neocortex, or rational brain, goes offline and the sympathetic nervous system takes over, engaging survival instincts such as fight or flight. This internal mechanism is totally natural and not in our control. It puts the body on high alert; pupils can get large, and heart rate can increase. Not all parts of the brain are fully online at this time. The hippocampus stops its function of storing memories and begins pumping cortisol into the body, so memories can get stuck in the limbic system instead of going where they're normally stored. This is why memories of events can be distorted, the sequence of things may be out of order, and certain elements may be missing entirely. Some details may be crystal clear, like the color of the car that hit you in an accident and that the road was gravel, but other details may be missing, such as which street it happened on or what day or time it was.

The repercussions experienced by victims after an event may seem strange to an observer. They can range from hysterical to emotionless or numb. They may seem hypervigilant, be easily startled, or catatonic. It's often much easier for a victim-survivor to recall how they felt at the time of the event rather than details, though they may not be able to feel the emotions because they're emotionally dissociated. These are normal responses, and are the body's and brain's way of taking care of us.

Trauma can change the structure of the brain and how it functions. Because we don't see the wound, like we can when it's on the surface of our bodies, the effects of the harm can easily go unnoticed and untreated. Brain scans of those who suffered abuse or have PTSD are dramatically different from "normal" scans; you can see the parts of the brain that are under or overdeveloped. Wounds of the body will show up as cuts and bruises. Psychological wounds show up in behaviors.

Trauma memories are encoded in the brain differently than regular memories. As I understand it, they're stored on the right side—where creativity and emotions live— near the primal section of the brain called the amygdala.

A person's ability to interact with a traumatic memory is different too. A regular memory can be recalled with both sides of the brain. The left side, where linear thinking and higher reasoning live, is accessible. You remember something, maybe even have emotions around it, but you know it's a memory because both sides of the brain have fired up.

But because of where the trauma memory is stored, and only one side of the brain is engaged, victim-survivors can get caught in a kind of emotional memory loop. The memory doesn't progress to where long-term memories are stored, and the trauma can be relived repeatedly because of it.

When a victim-survivor is "triggered" and a traumatic memory is engaged, it's as if they get pulled into that memory. The body cannot differentiate the memory from a real-time event because the left side of the brain—the logic part—isn't connected to the memory, so the body responds as if the event is occurring in the moment. The person may become terrified when there's no actual danger.

~ Fight, Flight, Freeze, and Appease ~

A trauma response is a normal reaction to extraordinary circumstances. We go through our days interacting with the world, and most of the time we cope with whatever is thrown at us. But sometimes, unexpected or dangerous things occur that cause a more primal reaction. At that point, the amygdala kicks in, which is where our fear responses live, and stress hormones are released into the body through the sympathetic nervous system. The four categories of automatic responses to fear are: fight, flight, freeze, and appease. We don't get to decide which one of them will engage, it just happens.

Most people are familiar with the term "fight or flight." The term "freeze" was added to the lexicon a few decades ago, increasing our understanding of the mental and physical reactions to danger. It makes sense—just think of a deer freezing in headlights. "Appease" or "Fawn" is a newer addition. The Sexual Trauma and Abuse Center in Kansas has an excellent pamphlet about the neurobiology of trauma that describes it this way:

> Appease refers to accommodation, where the person's brain and body respond by going along with the violence or initiating interactions as a way to minimize further violence. Victim-survivors who experience freeze or appease are often confused as to why they respond in that way, but the neurobiology of trauma reminds us that all of these responses are normal and part of our brain and body's survival mechanism.

In extreme circumstances, we have very little control over how we respond to danger. Our response may even be the opposite of what we would do in less threatening situations. There's a stigma attached to Freeze and Appease modes because they're considered weak by some uninformed people. In reality, these survival modes are just as important as their more active counterparts and can prevent harm or save lives. All four modes are natural instincts, and an individual does them all in different ways and to different degrees depending on circumstances.

When someone around me is in danger or gets hurt, I go into fight mode and spring into action. I'm the kind of person who would run toward a burning building to see how I could help, not flee from it. But for most of my life, when someone came after me in a sexually threatening way, I tended to freeze or appease.

~ Being Triggered and Post Traumatic Stress ~

triggered[3]
adjective
: (of a mechanism) activated by a trigger. "a triggered alarm"
: (of a response) caused by particular action, process, or situation. "a triggered memory of his childhood"

The term "triggered" has been overused and stripped of its impact. A food commercial that ignites your desire to get that food is a rather benign state of being triggered. I'm using the term here to describe what it feels like to have a post-traumatic stress episode due to a triggered memory.

Post-Traumatic Stress Disorder (PTSD) didn't appear in the *Diagnostic and Statistical Manual of Mental Disorders* (DSM) until 1980. For professionals who deal with trauma survivors— police, legal, and medical professionals—there's still a lot to learn. The term "disorder" is still debated by psychologists.

---

[3] Oxford Languages

PTSD is a mental and physical condition that occurs after a person experiences or witnesses an emotionally overwhelming event. Symptoms can surface months or even years later and can be short-term—lasting weeks to months—or chronic, lasting years. Symptoms vary from person to person and the intensity can change over time, for better or worse. They can include but aren't limited to; flashbacks, nightmares, severe anxiety, panic attacks, dissociation, memory problems, difficulty experiencing positive emotions, a feeling of emotional numbness, and self-destructive behavior.

For most of my life, I experienced disruptive behaviors in varying degrees of intensity having no clue that what I was experiencing was undiagnosed PTSD due to complex trauma. My symptoms started when I was little, so as far as I was concerned it was just the way things were—I felt broken and figured I'd stay that way.

When I get triggered by memories of past trauma, sometimes it feels like I'm physically back in that memory, like I'm transported back in time to the genesis of the trauma. I have no control over when this happens because my amygdala gets hijacked, and I'm in an altered state. Triggers for me can be smells, sounds, seeing someone or hearing a name that reminds me of past harm, driving through certain areas of town, even certain times of the year or the day. I begin to function more primally, and logic is irrelevant.

Believe me, if trauma survivors could just "get over it," we would. It's not fun to relive past traumas or have them control your life. Soldiers who have experienced combat have no desire to feel like they want to jump out of their skin when a firecracker goes off. Thankfully, PTSD is treatable, and I've found much relief in recent years through skilled accompaniment. If you experience PTSD, there is help. Please reach out to a therapist with experience treating this condition.

~ Healing Modalities ~

There are many types of therapy, but not all of them work well for trauma healing. Everyone is different, and what worked for one person may be harmful to another. You may need to try a few different kinds to find what is best for you. When searching, I'd recommend looking for someone who uses the following approaches that address the mind-body connection as it pertains to trauma: Trauma Focused[4], Narrative[5], AIR Network[6], Somatic[7], or EMDR[8]. If you're searching for a therapist online—on a website such as Psychologytoday.com— using the following keywords for specialties can help you narrow your search— anxiety, depression, trauma, childhood trauma, adolescent trauma, adult trauma, PTSD. If you're interested in learning more about the mind-body connection and trauma, you may find the Polyvagal Theory[9] and Neuroception[10] worth investigating.

---

[4] Trauma-focused (TF) psychotherapy uses different techniques to help people process traumatic experiences. Some involve visualizing, talking or thinking about the traumatic memory. Others focus on changing unhelpful beliefs about the trauma. PTSD-va.data.socrata.com

[5] A trauma narrative exposes the person to memories of the experience in a safe environment and helps them reframe the experience so the client can reclaim their power and autonomy. Crafting a this narrative helps clients to overcome the painful memories associated with the experience through the power of storytelling. Therapybrands.com

[6] Adaptive Internal Relational (AIR) Network therapy is a neuro-developmental, competency-based model of therapy primarily used to help people heal from past trauma and neglect. AIR Network Therapy places value on understanding the neurology associated with trauma and development. Turningleaftherapy.org

[7] Somatic trauma therapy is a type of intervention that encourages you to work through traumatic experiences and chronic stress by focusing on the physical body. Verywellhealth.com

[8] EMDR (Eye Movement Desensitization and Reprocessing) is a psychotherapy that enables people to heal from the symptoms and emotional distress that are the result of disturbing life experiences. Emdr.com

[9] Polyvagal Theory emphasizes the role the autonomic nervous system - especially the vagus nerve - plays in regulating our health and behavior. Polyvagalinstitute.org

[10] Neuroception: The term "Neuroception" describes how neural circuits distinguish whether situations or people are safe, dangerous, or life threatening. Eric.ed.gov

~ Trauma-Informed Care ~

In the simplest terms, being trauma-informed means paying attention to the whole human being, understanding and considering the nature of trauma, how we are all affected by it to some degree, and making choices that don't cause further harm to someone suffering from trauma.

Trauma-informed practices include:

- Creating safe spaces where people can be seen and heard.
- Being trustworthy in your actions, and transparent with information.
- Empowering someone to have a voice and autonomy in their choices.
- Being sensitive to, and recognizing, potential cultural, historical or gender issues that may cause a person discomfort or pain.

Thankfully, trauma-informed care practices are starting to be taught to those in the helping professions: clinicians, doctors and nurses, police, firefighters, etc. These folks are in constant contact with people in pain or stressful situations. Knowing how trauma affects the brain and behaviors allows caregivers and front-line workers to mitigate the potential to re-traumatize someone, and how to help them if they are dysregulated or disassociating.

This kind of knowledge and care shouldn't be exclusive to people in public service and the caring professions; everyone should pay attention to the needs of someone who is struggling emotionally.

~ Dysregulation and Dissociation~

Dysregulated nervous system[11]
A dysregulated nervous system is defined as an imbalance between the sympathetic and parasympathetic systems. It pres-

---

[11] Charliehealth.com

ents psychological, physical, or cognitive malfunctioning and imbalance which may inhibit normal functioning and the capacity to regulate responses.

dissociation[12]
noun
: the separation of whole segments of the personality or of discrete mental processes from the mainstream of consciousness or of behavior

When I'm emotionally triggered, my physical body can experience dysregulation. My brain stops using both sides. The right side, where trauma memories live, goes into high gear. If you think about the body as a machine, when everything is working properly, the engine purrs right along. A dysregulated system coughs and sputters because something in the machine is off balance.

When dysregulation happens in people, it can show up in a variety of ways. The body stops regulating properly, mental and emotional functions are interrupted, a person's heart rate might skyrocket, and breathing patterns can change. Fortunately, doing something that requires repeated bilateral movements such as going for a long walk engages both sides of the brain and can kick-start the left side into operation so the cogs can start moving properly again.

When triggers happen to me and my body dysregulates, sometimes I dissociate too. I feel as if I'm emotionally disconnected from my body. Memories can flood my brain rapidly, overwhelming me, and my emotions shut off. A memory can also fragment, becoming less accessible. My surroundings might feel unfamiliar or frightening. My brain sometimes gets so foggy I have a difficult time concentrating. Such an episode can be mild—lasting only until I'm able to find regulation again—or it can go on for days. Sometimes it lasts even longer depending on the circumstances. In extreme cases, it can cause a panic attack or post-traumatic stress event.

---

[12] Merriam-Webster.com

~ Toxic Stress ~

Stress is another one of those words that can be overused and misunderstood. It can mean many things and show up in a variety of ways. Feeling stressed is normal, we all experience it at one time or another.

There are three basic kinds of stress: positive, tolerable, and toxic. Positive stress is when your stress hormones kick in and your heart rate goes up. It's brief and goes away when the stressful situation is over. Tolerable stress is more intense but still temporary. It happens when a stressful situation is ongoing. If you have a good emotional support system, you can tolerate this level of stress much better.

Toxic Stress is ongoing. It can be found in those who live with physical or emotional abuse, neglect, extreme poverty, racism, have a caregiver who is mentally ill, or are exposed to ongoing violence. Toxic stress can diminish the body's ability to turn off the stress response, leaving a person in an ongoing state of fight or flight.

Toxic Stress is a treatable condition. Unaddressed Toxic Stress can have long-term medical consequences, including but not limited to sleep issues, stomach pain, headaches, muscle aches, anxiety and depression, trouble concentrating, and a weakened immune system.

~ Adverse Childhood Experiences ~

When children are exposed to emotional, mental, physical, or sexual abuse it can literally change their brain and alter the trajectory of their lives. Growing up is complicated under any circumstance. When trauma is added to the mix, it can seize the brain's ability to develop normally. Parts of us can freeze in the development process while we advance normally in other ways.

In the mid-1990s the Center for Disease Control and Kaiser Permanente conducted a study on Adverse Childhood Experiences (ACEs). The study found a direct link between elevated ACE scores and chronic diseases, employment challenges, and incarceration in adulthood.

ACEs are traumatic events and life situations that occur between the ages of zero and seventeen. Examples include but aren't limited to violence, abuse or neglect, witnessing violence, or the death of a family member. A child's environment will greatly affect how they process traumatic events. If a child lives in an unstable home affected by alcoholism, drug addiction, or mental health issues, or they have an incarcerated parent, the child will be more deeply affected by trauma than if they were in a stable situation. A child does not even need to remember a traumatic experience to be affected by it.

ACEs show how long-lasting the effects of childhood trauma are, and how they affect behaviors, such as smoking, drug and alcohol abuse, and physical and mental outcomes later in life. Bottom line: what we experience as children affects us as adults. People with higher ACEs scores have shorter life spans, and higher rates of depression and anxiety, obesity, diabetes, heart and lung disease, stroke, and cancer.

Knowing your ACEs score can be a useful thing when processing trauma. It can give you a roadmap to discover what is at the center of difficulties you're experiencing. To learn more about ACEs testing and prevention, visit the Center for Disease Control website[13].

~ Secondary Trauma and Compassion Fatigue ~

Someone's traumatic experience doesn't end at the borders of their body and mind. The residuals can be felt deeply by the people around them, internalizing the trauma as if it's their own. Vicarious, or secondary trauma, can happen to spouses, children, friends and family, therapists, advocates, educators, medical personnel, police, and people working in the judicial system.

For those who were subjected to complex trauma, like chronic abuse, systemic oppression, genocide, and war, research shows the effects of trauma can be passed on through generations as secondary trauma, showing up in descendants as compromised psychological and physical health.

---

[13] https://www.cdc.gov/violenceprevention/aces/index.html

Being exposed to the emotional fallout of a traumatized person can be damaging in the long term for those who care about and for them. They can get saturated and overwhelmed with the weight of being present to so much stress, which can create compassion fatigue.

compassion fatigue[14]
noun
: indifference to charitable appeals on behalf of those who are suffering, experienced as a result of the frequency or number of such appeals.

I came across a woman in a park who was in a panic because her boyfriend had stopped breathing. I called 911 and was instructed to do chest compressions until the ambulance showed up, so I did. The police and an ambulance arrived within minutes, the EMT's rushing in with all speed and focus. The lead EMT came in to see what was happening, looked at the man's eyes, announced to the team, "Overdose," and everything changed. There was no more rushing. This man was still alive, but the urgency to assist him had completely disappeared. I was furious.

Looking back, I have a clearer understanding of what was happening; those first responders were experiencing compassion fatigue. Addicts overdose frequently, police officers and EMTs see it every day on the job. They might even see the same people multiple times. They work every day to save lives, and when they see someone they perceive to be self-inflicting a wound, it can make them really frustrated, which causes them to compartmentalize, and they detach from their emotions. They save their caring for people who aren't abusing themselves. This is what compassion fatigue can look like. It's so sad because even drug addicts deserve our compassion.

Those who deal with survivors of trauma all the time need to take care of themselves so they can be their most resourced selves when doing their jobs. Having a healthy work-life balance can help

---

[14] Oxford languages

prevent burnout. We have to be able to step away from the stress and recharge ourselves.

If you're suffering from this kind of trauma, put yourself at the top of the list of things to take care of, and reach out for help.

~ The Downgrading of Trauma ~

Downgrading trauma means minimizing the truth of an experience to lessen the emotional impact. Victim-survivors do this to themselves, but we also do it to each other because it's hard to be present to the intensity of emotional and psychological wounds of trauma. We do this by downplaying an event itself, "It really wasn't that bad," or diminishing the experience of someone else, "Why are you making such a big deal over this?"

Downgrading our trauma can make it easier to bear the weight of it, but it's also damaging to our psyches. It allows emotional wounds to fester in the darkness. Not talking about our trauma gives it strength, and it can have power over how we participate in our lives. Seeing our experiences for what they are allows us to process our thoughts and emotions so healing can happen.

~ Sexual Abuse ~

All abuse inflicted by another human being is painful and leaves emotional scars, but because society teaches us that our genitals define who we are, even more so than the culture we come from or the color of our skin, victim-survivors of sexual violence experience a psychological wound that strikes at the very core of their humanity. That kind of violation can dramatically change the way a person sees themselves and how they relate to the world around them in fundamental ways. The effects of harm will vary from person to person depending on the circumstances of their lives.

Sexual violence can happen to anyone. It doesn't discriminate. The most vulnerable members of society, such as children, the elderly, women, LGBTQ[15], BIPOC[16], disabled, and differently-abled people; all experience sexual violence at higher rates. Perpetrators seek out victims who are vulnerable because they're less likely to report the abuse. Men are often the abusers, but they can also be abused. [17] Women and those who identify as female are most often abused, but they can also be an abuser. And children can be victims or offenders.

To learn more about the statistics of sexual violence, visit RAINN. org

~ Ready for Take Off ~

We're currently living in a highly stressful environment. We're forced on a daily basis to confront challenges in our little corner of the world, in addition to frightening global issues. Unless you're living under a rock, it's nearly impossible to avoid seeing dreadful news headlines or having challenging conversations about climate issues, public health concerns, political strife, and cultural conflicts. The people on the frontlines of these issues bear a lot of the emotional weight while they do their jobs or fight for change. Unresolved trauma adds to the compound stresses of society.

Recognizing the scope of trauma on the planet, and understanding why it's critical that we address the impact are of the utmost importance. All too often unresolved trauma sits at the center of our relationships and affects the way we interact with one another and see ourselves, whether we're aware of it or not. Issues that arise can reduce productivity and efficiency at home or work. The benefits of

---

[15] LGBTQ- Lesbian, Gay, Bisexual, Transgender and Queer/or Questioning- this acronym sometimes includes IA+, meaning Intersex, asexual, and all other possible distinctions regarding sexual identity and gender.

[16] BIPOC- Black, Indigenous, and People of Color- This acronym is problematic for some because they have a hard time finding themselves in the distinctions because they may be more than one, or they don't agree with the labels. If someone who is not white bodied expresses discomfort with this acronym, ask them what they prefer.

[17] 98% of perpetrators are men https://sbstesa.org/resources/myths-truths/#toggle-id-13

healing unresolved trauma are immeasurable, because the smallest move in a healthy direction can create ripples of positive change, in every aspect of our lives, and affect those around us in a positive way. Why would we not put our energy towards this bountiful endeavor?

The work of personal growth can be extremely challenging. Just as it's important to have a spotter when doing weight training, it's valuable to have someone walk with you as you learn new skills. The exercises in this book will have you digging around in your memories and experiences and will likely cause you to bump up against some unresolved issues. Doing it alone is not only difficult, but it can also be unhealthy. I encourage you to avoid isolating yourself emotionally or socially while doing this work. Ask for accompaniment from friends or family, a trusted therapist, or a religious or spiritual advisor. Go to the people who will give you the best support for your needs, not to someone who doesn't support or understand what you're trying to do—as the saying goes, "don't go to the hardware store for raisins."

Questions to ask yourself before moving on:

- Did I learn anything new about trauma or gain a deeper understanding of something?
- Do I downgrade my own trauma experiences or those of others?
- Have I ever experienced secondary trauma or compassion fatigue?

If you are struggling:

This book is not a replacement for therapy. *If you're having severe feelings of anxiety, depression, or find yourself overwhelmed by the things that come up in you as you read, stop reading, and find help. Talk to a therapist before deciding to do the exercises in this book because they can trigger things that you don't expect, and if you're already in a fragile state, you may need to wait until you're in a better mental and emotional place.*

Some trauma is too painful to revisit without skilled accompaniment. For those whose experience was so painful you fear even talking about it, there are ways to heal trauma that don't require discussing what happened, such as Somatic Therapy or EMDR. There are times when it's better to address symptoms rather than dissect the source of the trauma. This decision should be determined in therapy with a professional who is highly skilled at treating complex trauma.

If you're working with a therapist who isn't addressing your concerns, doesn't feel like the right fit for you, or a therapist has burned you in the past, there are many options available to you. I encourage you to find someone who is right for you and can give you the care you deserve.

For those in the BIPOC community, finding a culturally competent therapist, who understands the added layers of cultural issues, will be vital to you feeling seen and heard.

If you suffer from compound or complex trauma, or are experiencing untreated PTSD symptoms, please take care of yourself and seek professional assistance. It's not a sign of weakness to ask for help. It's a sign of strength and personal awareness to recognize that you need assistance.

Chapter Three

Awareness

From the get-go, humans start developing a belief system. It precedes the ability to understand language. When we start to develop the ability to focus our eyes, we start to make decisions about the faces we see. *That face is good— comforting. That face is unknown— scary.* This information starts to be collected immediately.

As our understanding grows, and we learn more, we continue to make decisions about the world and our place in it. However, the foundation of our belief system is based on the limited cognitive ability of a child. Our brains aren't fully developed until we're in our mid-twenties. By the time we reach adulthood we've developed a complicated set of beliefs, most of them subconscious, and many of them false. Our beliefs were cemented in our brains at an early age, yet we live our adult lives based on them.

Sometimes we get stuck in certain beliefs and patterns of behavior that made sense when we were children that don't work in the adult world, but we don't necessarily recognize them as unhealthy—it's just the way the world is. Our awareness of these beliefs can grow and evolve as we age, and we can develop new beliefs based on updated information. And thank goodness for that— I don't want to live my life based on the decisions I made as a seven-year-old.

As adults, many of us never look back at what makes up our belief systems because it can be very painful, even if we experienced a relatively easy upbringing. If we experienced trauma as a child, there's a huge set of additional complications which make it even harder to evolve our thinking, including the fact that children often don't recognize harm when it happens to them, so they don't even know there's something to be healed. Or their life is so filled with harm they just see it as the way the world functions, and don't recognize it can be different. Trauma can be the bedrock of a belief system.

I first came across the 3 A's—Awareness, Acceptance, and Action—when learning about Twelve Step Recovery[18]. They've helped me identify destructive patterns in my life, to see them for what they are, and have allowed me to make different choices. To me, the 3 A's are the core to shifting negative thinking, but you can't have lasting and profound change without all three—and they need to be in that order. How can you take action to change something you don't accept as a problem? How can you accept something that you aren't aware exists?

The wisdom of the 3 A's, in practicality, are simple concepts. This is not to say that they are easy to implement. Waking up, seeing the truth, and taking action is hard work.

I'm someone who doesn't like to struggle with the process of mastering something. I've been blessed with the ability to learn things quickly, and if I can't, I don't want to bother. I want to absorb and feel competent immediately, and when I don't, I feel stupid, weak, and unworthy. There were many challenges for me in absorbing the 3 A's, but thankfully I set aside my perfectionism and took the time to let them sink in. Over time I've acquired some ability to unearth the gems these tools can uncover and apply their value to my life.

It's my sincerest hope that you'll find some proficiency with the concept and implementation of the 3 A's by reading this book and doing the exercises suggested. The beginning of this book is dedicated to understanding them because they're the foundation for all the layers that follow.

Every now and then, someone does or says something around me they recognize as "off," like an off-the-cuff comment about child abuse or sexual violence, and they look at me with horror and apprehension, not sure how I'll respond. "I'm so sorry, I forgot who I was talking to. I hope that wasn't offensive. I can't believe I just said that."

---

[18] Twelve step recovery programs include Alcoholic Anonymous (AA), Al-anon and Al-ateen for friends and families of substance users, Overeaters Anonymous, Narcotics Anonymous, and many others.

I always assure them that I'm fine and I recognize the process of awareness is ever-evolving in each of us. "Thank you for seeing me," I say.

The fact that it even registers with people is important. I'm the face of someone who talks about childhood sexual abuse as a personal experience, which I've chosen to make public, and I tap into certain neuropathways in other people because of that. I'm totally okay with it. They may feel like they fumbled, but for me, it helps me see that I've succeeded in helping them be more aware. I hope the experience of saying something and realizing it was off base or bad timing, will filter into their other relationships, and they'll be more aware as they move through their lives.

Many years ago, I heard the term "The first step is the hardest." I don't remember what it was in reference to, it seems like a saying I've always known. But just because I heard something a long time ago, doesn't mean that I understood it. In theory, it makes sense. Progressing from a position of stillness to motion can be incredibly difficult, nearly impossible depending on the circumstances. I liken it to trying to drive a stick shift after learning to drive on an automatic. It doesn't feel natural, it's hard to find the right muscle coordination to make all of the moving parts sing harmoniously and get that blasted car rolling without killing the engine. Many people just give up, or never even try, because it's so much easier to just do what you've always done than to do it differently, even if that new way might ultimately be better.

People who have suffered from trauma find ways to cope, and to keep moving. The first time I was sexually assaulted I made decisions about myself, about the world around me, and how I would engage with it, based on a child's understanding of what happened to me. I was wounded in ways I didn't come to fully realize for a very long time, and I was way too young to get the significance of how it arranged my view of the world. And yet, I was in motion. My vehicle was moving but I was on automatic pilot regarding my sexuality, my relationship to intimacy, and what I thought a woman should be. It was more than thirty-five years before I'd take a real step towards a true understanding of these things, and take control of the wheel.

For a long time, I figured if I just pretended the horrible things that happened to me weren't a big deal, they wouldn't be. Sadly, that's not really how trauma works—the effects live in our bodies whether or not we want to acknowledge it. This method of coping worked for me at first—denial can be powerful. But eventually, the symptoms of my unresolved trauma became unmanageable.

The downgrading I'd done around my experiences made thinking about them more tolerable, or easier to push away, but it caused me to shut down emotionally and I developed a skewed perspective of myself. I didn't make the connection that my unhealthy behaviors, sleep issues, and suicidal ideation were linked to trauma. I mean, come on, don't we all avoid conflict at all costs, struggle with insomnia, and want to drive our cars off bridges? No?

Sometimes we don't recognize the need for change. It's like we're asleep and change doesn't register as necessary until we're made painfully aware of how bad things have been. Have you ever woken up from a deep sleep shivering only to realize that you have no covers on you? It's like that. If you're willing to embrace these concepts, the 3 A's can transform your experience, like pulling a warm blanket over yourself to take the chill away. They can warm you, thaw you, and bring you from frozen to fluid. How dramatic the change is depends on how willing you are to be transformed, but understanding them can alter your life.

I know people who believe digging around in their past only brings up pain and doesn't make them feel better. I understand that. My first therapist was not helpful to me because she didn't give me anything to do with the pain I was uncovering in our sessions. She would listen, but the most she would say was, "That must have been really painful." Or when I'd ask her what I should do about it she would reply, "What do *you* think you should do?" What I wanted to do when she said that was smack her face. Talk therapy is useful to some people, and if you're one of them, I'm so glad you find relief from it. For me, I needed more.

Awareness is the first step to addressing unresolved trauma, but what does it really mean?

awareness[19]
noun
: *the quality or state of being aware: knowledge and understanding that something is happening or exists*

This definition leads me to the idea that you need to be awake to be aware. To be awake on an emotional level requires a willingness to be present to reality, not just the physical reality of existing on the planet, but the reality of what lies below the surface of our conscious mind. We need to be willing to look into the darkness. To pick up our memories, like a log in the forest, and see what's living underneath.

I picture the place in my mind where my painful memories live as a pond, the kind that has a muddy bottom, and my most painful memories live in the deep sediment. When I mentally visit these bad experiences, the sediment gets stirred up, the water gets murky—it can be very dysregulating. There's debris in there I'd love to get rid of entirely, but these things are part of my history and can't be erased. When I step away from those memories the sediment settles, and the ugliness of those experiences floats back down to the bottom.

The bad news is that the potential for disturbing that sediment is always there—those things that live in the shadows of that pond are part of me and can easily be triggered.

The good news is that understanding how I've been affected by the things in my past returns power that was taken from me, giving me the ability to respond to things in the present moment, instead of just reacting out of old habits and a belief system that no longer serves me.

---

[19] Merriam-Webster.com

~ What Do I Believe? ~

Everyone has core beliefs—things they believe to be empirically[20] true. A positive belief could be something like "everything happens for a reason." Core beliefs help us in our daily lives to keep a perspective that's useful to our mental wellbeing. A negative or false belief could be "I never do anything right." These kinds of beliefs keep us trapped in negative thinking.

I don't like stirring up things that are uncomfortable, but it's useful. Through the years, with the help of friends and skilled therapists, I've mapped out what's lurking at the bottom of my mental pond and taken an inventory, which provides clues as to why I walk through the world the way I do. Before I did that emotional investigation, I was at the mercy of the things hidden at the bottom of my pond.

I used to think the term "knowledge is power" meant I needed to be smart in order to do something, that the smartest ones get to wield the power. That's not how I see it today. I believe it means that information gives you the ultimate power of *choice*. How can you make a choice about something if you don't have information? It's the only power we really have in this world: personal choice. We don't even have the power to stop a single thought from happening in our brains. They're like farts— they just happen. But we have a choice about what we do with our thoughts.

Awareness can happen in a flash, like waking from a dream. Or it can happen slowly, like a limb regaining feeling after you've sat in the wrong position for too long. As uncomfortable as waking up can be, like the prickly feeling when blood starts flowing back into a numb leg, I prefer the freedom I've gained, to choose how I participate in my life, over the unconscious, numbly automatic way I was living. I'm now in the driver's seat of my life, not a back-seat driver to my False Core Beliefs— more on this in a moment.

Finding the cause of a painful thing can in and of itself make

---

[20] Empirically: adverb; with a basis in or reliance on information obtained through observation, experiment, or experience. Merriam-Webster.com

you feel better. In my early twenties, I was talking to a friend about this feeling I'd get in my chest. I said, "...you know, when your heart flutters like a butterfly and you get chest pain," as if that was how it was for everyone. My friend looked at me with deep concern. "No," she said, "I don't know what that's like. You should see a doctor about that."

Before then I had no reason to be afraid of this feeling. It had always been there, so I assumed it was normal. Now I had concerns. After my friend's comment, when this feeling would happen, I'd get scared and my blood pressure would rise, which would exacerbate the problem. Long story short, after being misdiagnosed with a mitral valve prolapse, years of worsening symptoms, and feeling like I was crazy because doctors seemed to think it was all in my head, I was properly diagnosed in my mid-thirties by a cardiologist I'd never seen before. At my first consult, he looked me straight in the eye and said, "I want you to know that I believe you. We're going to figure out what's going on with you."

My eyes filled with tears of relief. Just having someone see me and acknowledge my experience as *real* made me feel better. It turns out I have an extremely rare birth defect, a deformation of the heart called Epstein's Anomaly— a displaced tri-cuspid valve—only about one percent of heart patients have it. Knowing what is at the root of the problem and that I'm not having a heart attack helps me stay calm, and the symptoms don't accelerate from amped-up anxiety. Medication helps control the symptoms, but more importantly, it helps me just knowing what the cause is.

More often though, awareness alone isn't enough to address or transform an issue. It's only a step in the right direction, not the thing that affects true change.

Stopping at the discovery stage can be problematic. Going through the process of identifying the root of an emotional or behavioral problem and then doing nothing to address it is akin to being diagnosed with an infection and not taking an antibiotic to get rid of it. With severe infections, if you don't take the antibiotic, it can not only be extremely painful, but it can also kill you.

Not addressing buried complex trauma when it surfaces can be deadly. One of the victims who was abused when we were children at CTC lived a lifetime of chemical dependency and depression because of it. After the CTC lawsuits went public, one of his friends encouraged him to file a lawsuit himself. When his unresolved complex trauma was triggered and came to the surface, he went into an emotional tailspin. He died of an overdose not long afterward. This is the reality of what can happen when we don't move *through* unresolved trauma, and it reinforces the importance of having skilled accompaniment when exploring it. When addressing the effects of trauma, awareness isn't enough.

I started having sleep issues at a young age. One of my early memories happened around the age of six; I woke up to the noise of something flying around my room in the darkness. It flew right by my head and I was terrified. I opened my mouth to scream, but I was so scared no sound came out. It turned out it was a bat that had gotten into the house through the attic or the chimney—a recurring problem in that old house. But after that experience, I always needed a light on to fall asleep, usually the light in my closet with the door cracked a little, to keep the monsters at bay.

Starting around this time I began having recurring nightmares. Sometimes small details were different, but it generally went like this: I'd be walking down an alley at night, the pavement and tall brick walls on either side of me were wet from rain, and I could see dim light reflecting on the slick surfaces. I'd hear a noise coming from a tin garbage can, and when I'd lift the lid to see what was making the noise, expecting to see Oscar the Grouch from Sesame Street, I'd discover that it was a secret passage to an underground room. I'd climb into the garbage can and descend a rickety ladder to a secret hideaway. I could hear voices of bad men and knew I shouldn't be there, but when I'd turn to leave the ladder would be gone. The bad men would see me and start coming towards me. I had no way to escape, and I'd start to cry, knowing they were going to hurt me. Thankfully, I'd wake up crying before they got to me. I had variations of this dream weekly for about ten years. I don't know what the genesis of this specific dream is; it may precede my memories, but the dream is still clear after all these years.

After I was sexually assaulted at the age of ten, the dream advanced from a threat of harm to a threat of rape. And in addition to needing a light on, I stopped being able to fall asleep without some kind of sound to occupy my brain—a fan, music, or a television with the volume low. Without that, my thoughts would keep me awake for hours, my mind spinning like there was a little hamster in my brain that just wouldn't get off that wheel without a distraction. And after the assault, it wasn't just fear that the men in my recurring nightmare would hurt me, it was that they would rape me.

It didn't occur to me that my sleep problems from early child hood were exacerbated because of being sexually assaulted. It's not unusual for children to have sleep issues but they typically grow out of the problem as they age. For me, they amplified and endured into adulthood— I still have trouble sleeping without a distracting sound. When I purchased my first television, I got one with a timer that would turn it off after one, two, or three hours so it wouldn't run all night long. The worst nights were when I was still awake after the three-hour timer shut the TV off—I'd have to fire it up again. As an adult, I graduated from a closet light through a cracked door to nightlights or small decorative lamps in my bedroom and around the house so it would never be completely dark.

It wasn't until well into my adulthood when I put the pieces together that my sleep issues had a cause other than just a bad night's sleep. The giant neon sign I needed to finally put the pieces together were nightmares involving the people who had harmed me, and physical paralysis if I was touched while sleeping. Before that, I was "asleep" to the fact that my sleep issues had a genesis. Awareness around it was the first step towards doing something about it.

Some people walk through life with no negative self-talk, they love everything about life and don't understand how people can't see the bright side of things[21]. In my experience, these people are extremely rare. If you're one of them, welcome, and bless your fuzzy little heart. I love that you exist in the world, and I admire your level of positivity. I'm not wired like you, but I appreciate you. I hope you're finding useful information here, to help you understand those of us who just don't process like you do.

For the rest of you, I can't promise you that this process will work for you. I can attest to my own experience, which shows me that investigating my belief system was liberating. It was like waking up from a horrible dream and seeing that things could be different. I was able to shake off shackles that have kept me bound to a game I didn't know I was playing; with a set of rules I didn't know existed. I went from a place of constantly reacting to the world around me to recognizing that I have a choice about it and being able to choose a response instead.

The very sad reality is that most people go through their entire lives and never become aware of what is going on beneath the surface of their own thoughts. They repeat harmful behavior, not understanding why, and are unable to change.

~ What Do I Think? ~

When I first started doing this kind of work, it was sometimes hard to identify what exactly I was thinking, let alone what the False Core Belief was hiding behind it. It was hard to determine what thoughts were mine and what was fed to me earlier in life. I also have a really strong coping mechanism of forgetting. Denial is a very powerful thing that can keep me from seeing what's going on in my head or knowing what I'm feeling. Some of us spend our lives emulating the thoughts and habits of the people who raised us. We parrot sayings or ideology we were entrenched in as children, or in school.

Everything that happens to us imprints in our bodies— the good,

---

[21] I feel it's important to acknowledge that unrelenting cheerfulness, or "bright-siding" everything, can be a form of avoidance. I've been there myself.

the bad, the ugly. We may not cognitively remember the details of what happens to us, but we have a physical memory that accompanies the experience— often connected to a smell, a touch, or a sound. Our brains record it all. Because of this, our bodies are excellent teachers. Even if you have no memory of an earlier experience, your sense memories can trigger feelings you don't consciously connect to a memory— a certain smell may make you happy or sad, and you don't know why.

Our bodies are designed to heal and protect us. When I get a cut, my body kicks into healing mode without me even trying. My blood thickens, a scab forms, new skin grows and the wound is healed. Sometimes my body goes into overdrive, creating a situation where too much of a good thing can be bad. An overabundance of calcium created a lump over a broken bone in my foot that aches when I'm on my feet too much.

With emotional wounds, my body does its best to heal me too. My brain has buried emotional trauma like a dog with a precious bone, hidden deeply so no one will find it. But just like the calcium deposit on my foot, the ache doesn't go away entirely. There came a point in my life when I could no longer deny the emotional ache of trauma and had to figure out what was going on. My body was my guide.

Shame often accompanies emotional trauma— the shame of what happened and how I dealt with it or didn't deal with it. But just as I can't blame my body for doing too good a job healing that bone, I shouldn't beat myself up for how I've coped with emotional trauma. My brain was doing the best it could to keep me safe and sane.

When I can't figure out what my thinking is, or I react to something in a way that is illogical or counterintuitive, I look to my feelings and my body to give me clues. I pay attention to where the sensations connected to what I'm feeling are rooted in my body— my stomach, my back, my shoulders. I pay attention to the quality of the feeling— does it ache, burn, tingle, is it tight or numb? I try to identify other times I've felt the same way and what was happening in my life at that time. This is often enough to fire up my neural network.

Another tool I've used stems from an exercise in *The Artist's Way* by Julia Cameron called Morning Pages. Writing down a stream-of-consciousness thought process can unblock your thinking, and clear away the clutter in your mind, allowing things that are sitting deeper to rise to the surface. Sit and write for five to ten minutes without stopping. Don't think, just write. Even if it's blah blah blah for an entire page—don't stop. Eventually, something should pop up that you didn't know you were thinking.

Once I've identified the thought, depending on what it is, I ask myself any number of the following questions:

- Is there someone I need to talk to about this? If so, who, and can I do that now?
- If the thought is connected to a memory, is there anything I need to do to take care of myself? Do I need more clarity? How can I get it?
- How is my thinking serving me today?
- How does this thought make me feel in my body? Are there other times I've felt this?
- Is this thought mine or one I've heard and claimed as mine?
- If this is an old thought, does this thinking feel relevant anymore? How is it serving me today?

This kind of internal expedition for someone new to it can be frustrating, bewildering, and even scary. It's best not to do this kind of work by yourself. As author Ann Lamott says, "My mind is a neighborhood I try not to go into alone." I'll share how you can find accompaniment later in this chapter.

~ Identifying False Core Beliefs ~

Identifying False Core Beliefs can release us from a belief system that has kept our negative thinking in the driver's seat of our lives— it's one of the most valuable things I've done in my healing journey. I'm so happy to share it with you here. A False Core Belief can be difficult to pin down. The following is a list of common False Core Beliefs, and each of these can have a thousand variations on the theme, unique to an individual:

- I'm unlovable.
- I never do anything right.
- There's something wrong with me.
- I'm bad.
- I'll never be successful.
- I'm not important.
- Everyone I love goes away.
- I'm responsible for everything.
- I'm not safe.
- I'm a fraud.
- I'm not enough.
- I'm an idiot.
- I'm worthless.
- I'm ugly.
- It's all my fault.
- I don't deserve to be alive.
- I'm better off alone.
- Nothing I do matters.

Early in my process, I found four False Core Beliefs that were embedded in me at a very young age. They are:

- I'm broken.
- I'm not important.
- The enjoyment of others is more important than my own.
- I'm not deserving.

Through the years I've been able to refine them and have added a couple. This is my list today:

- I'm broken and I can't be fixed.
- My needs are less important than the needs of others.
- I don't deserve _____ [fill in the blank: e.g., nice things, love, happiness, etc.]
- I'm not _____ enough [fill in the blank: e.g., good, pretty, skinny, etc.] Or, without a qualifier, *I'm* not enough.
- If people really knew me, they would go away.
- I'm stupid.

My False Core Beliefs boil down to these six thoughts. My negative self-talk lives in one of these six pots, just waiting for fertilizer. "I don't deserve" and "I'm not enough" are very closely related, but I've made the distinction for myself around the deserving piece because it's so prevalent for me it merits its own category.

When I first started looking at my False Core Beliefs, they were very hard to see. In fact, if you asked me about my life twenty-five years ago, I would have told you I had a happy childhood, had experienced a few bumps along the road but had escaped relatively unscathed, was a happily married mother of two and doing just fine, thank you very much.

I wasn't able to address some of the problems in my life, acknowledge the deep sadness I was experiencing, or tap into the sources of that sadness. I didn't see how numb I was emotionally. I'd spent so many years living without a full spectrum of feelings because of unresolved complex trauma, I didn't know what I was missing. In order for me to see what was true took a deep commitment to the process of discovery, and some skilled accompaniment to reflect back to me how I was participating in my own life.

A few years back, when my parents were still alive, it was pointed out to me that I'd "go away" emotionally for several days after being around them. It was described to me that my eyes would get distant, I was distracted from what I was doing, and unavailable emotionally for days. I know today that these are classic symptoms of PTSD. Honestly, I had no idea this was happening until it was brought to my attention. Then I started to see it for myself.

Through this work I've figured out the source of that distance and sadness—I'd been sexually assaulted at the age of ten, in my own bedroom, and I never told my parents. That secret created an emotional wall inside me, and it kept me from being fully present to my love for them. All of my False Core Beliefs had been triggered by being assaulted and it kept me frozen emotionally.

I'd been doing this work for almost two decades at that point and hadn't been able to see it for myself. Once I became aware of what I was doing, I did the investigative work to find the root of the problem. Afterward, I was able to be more present to my parents. The sadness didn't fully go away for a long time, but I was no longer at its mercy, and I found a new joy in being around them. My relationship with each of them was profoundly affected and we grew very close in the years before they died. It's unlikely I ever would have had that experience with them if someone close to me hadn't helped me see how I was acting.

The value of this process of discovery is incalculable, but it's not easy. You may find it difficult even getting started. This work is a bit like peeling an onion. It can take time to get through all of the layers, so be patient with yourself. And I suggest you not do it alone.

~ Processing Partner- Finding the Right Witness to your Process ~

We aren't meant to move through our lives alone. We're social creatures and benefit from accompaniment. But often the shame attached to psychological and emotional trauma keeps us isolated and we fear exposing the most private and delicate parts of ourselves. If you've spent years holding the weight of shame in isolation, then it's kept you from the invaluable gift of accompaniment. But don't worry. It's never too late for self-care.

To identify a False Core Belief, you have to do some internal searching. And it's better if you have a witness to your process. It's much easier to identify false beliefs if you're processing out loud with someone else that you trust. Not only will they see things that you don't, but they can reflect truths back to you that you're missing because your False Core Beliefs can get in the way and blind you from what's actually going on—they're tricky little buggers.

Professional athletes have coaches for a reason; because you can't always see what you're doing, and you need someone to give you a different perspective. A golf coach can help you see why you're slicing or shanking the ball. It's even more important to have that kind of outside assistance when dealing with something as important as your life and how you're participating in it.

Finding the right person to help you is crucial to your success, someone who will give it to you straight but take care of you in the process. You could ask a trusted friend, therapist, minister, or any-one who truly has your best interest at heart. Think of someone you would let remove a Band-Aid, who would ask you kindly if you're ready and how you want them to do it—a quick rip or a slow gentle peel—and they would do it exactly the way you asked.

You don't want the person who would say, "Buck up chum, grow a pair," rip off the Band-Aid and start pouring rubbing alcohol on you before you knew what hit you. Find the person who would say, "I'm sorry to tell you this, but that cut really needs stitches. I'll hold your hand while they stitch you up if you want me to." That's the per-son you want, because in a sense they'll be tending to your wounds, the less tangible ones that live near the delicate underbelly of your psyche.

Once you identify this processing partner for yourself, ask them if they'll help you with something important, and that it might take some time to accomplish. Tell them what you're doing and what you need them to do. Ask them to help you. If they decline, they aren't the right one to help you anyway. Move on and find the right one. If they say "I'm so honored that you would ask me. Of course, I'll help you," then you've hit the jackpot in your search. Tell them that their job is to bear witness to your process, to ask questions, and to reflect what they see and hear to you so you can see it for yourself. You're on a truth-finding excursion and they are your trusted assistant. Thank them and set up a time to meet. It would be beneficial to share this chapter of the book with them, so they understand what you're look-ing for and how they can help you find it.

For those reading this who have agreed to be a processing part-ner, thank you for saying yes. Your job is primarily to listen and ask questions. It's not up to you to name someone else's False Core Belief for them, you're here to help them name it for themselves. It might be blatantly obvious to you what's at the core because you have the priv-ilege of witnessing this process without the attachment of emotions, but let them find it. If they're really struggling to see it and you have words to suggest, to steer them in the right direction, offer them, but allow the person to find their own way to say it, using language that fits for them.

I highly recommend you meet face to face, either in person or via the internet. There's something about being able to feel a person's energy and look into their eyes that makes for a safe and healthy space for this delicate work. Do it in private because this can be dif-ficult and emotional. Take care of yourselves while you do this. Give yourselves the gift of privacy, so you can experience whatever feelings come up and share them without having to edit yourself. In other words, don't meet at a coffee shop to do this work. You don't need an audience for this.

~ Finding Gratitude ~

It can be overwhelming to do this work, so take care of yourself while you're doing it. Start small. This will take time. Don't try and do this in a stressful environment or when you have something that will be emotionally taxing right after. Poking around in our thinking can release a floodgate. If you haven't found someone to be your process-ing partner yet, do that first before doing this yourself, so that you have their support in every aspect of this mining expedition.

You'll be making a list of your thoughts, but before you go on a deep dive of discovery in your negative thought process, let's look at the positive. This will create something to buoy you up when you need it.

When I was in my saddest days, I was told to make a list of three things I was grateful for. This was laughable at first, not because I found it silly but because it was a struggle to find three things. But there was always something; usually my kids—and chocolate. This was enough to get me started and I could scrape up one more. Thankfully, today my list could go on and on.

Make a list of ten things you're grateful for. Go ahead and do that now. If this is a struggle, and you can't come up with ten things, or the entire list consists of inanimate objects, it's not time for you to go diving into your negative thoughts. This gratitude list is going to serve as a flotation device, and if you don't have enough positive elements to pump it up, you might get swamped when the water gets choppy. There's other work you need to do before you jump in here. Talk to someone about where you're at. I'll meet you back here when you're ready.

Once you have your gratitude list, soak it in. Feel it! Then take that list and put it up somewhere you can see it every day. I used to tape mine to the bookshelf next to my bed so it was the first thing I saw when I rolled out of bed in the morning. Once you have this personal flotation device, you can move on.

To identify your False Core Beliefs, you're going to go into the quarry of your thoughts and bring up some clumps of negativity in your thinking, which you can then begin to pick apart. Topics might include destructive self-talk that tumbles through your head or negative thinking that keeps you from seeing the positive aspects of yourself or your relationships, which can be with people, pets, or concepts such as capitalism, or ideals such as beauty.

If this kind of thought process isn't something you're used to doing it can be hard to even identify what you're thinking, good or bad. Listening to our thoughts can be very difficult and uncomfortable, even confusing. If this is the case for you, it might be useful to spend some time just paying attention to your thoughts and not writing anything down. Listening is a skill—it can be hard to listen when words are being spoken out loud, and listening to your thoughts can be even harder.

Identifying your positive thoughts and emotions as a starting place can be a way to tap into this part of your brain. Use your gratitude list if you want. As you think about good things, pay attention to where the accompanying emotion lives energetically in your body. My happy feelings usually live in my chest, negative feelings tend to manifest in my stomach. Just acknowledging where that energy is coming from can help reveal the thinking that surrounds the feeling.

If you don't feel ready to start writing, instead, go on a quiet walk or a ride, and just pay attention to the way the earth feels under your feet or how the wheels sound on the ground. How does it feel physically and emotionally? Can you find gratitude for your body and thank it for housing you all these years? Where does that gratitude live in you? Is it in your heart or somewhere else? Does it radiate like a warm light from your chest, does it sit firm in your belly like a peach pit? Recognizing these things is a gateway to finding the truth around your thinking. After you're done with this excursion, write about the experience and how gratitude for your body showed up. Or maybe you weren't able to find gratitude. If that's the case, you might need to spend more time with your gratitude list.

~ Identification Exercise ~

I'd like to acknowledge Mildred Frank, a popular speaker on the recovery circuit, for an exercise she created, which is part of the foundation of this process. I learned the basic step from her at a women's retreat many years ago and have expanded how I've used that tool.

Once you feel ready, and you have dedicated time set aside with a computer or pen in hand, you're going identify what you're unhappy about, a resentment, someone you're upset with. Eventually, you'll make a list, but for now, start small.

Pick something specific but not broad, like something someone did that upset you, instead of something complex like mistrust of the government. It could be something that happened last week, or when you were eight, anything, as long as you still feel the energy of the upset. The simpler the upset the easier it'll be to find what you're looking for. When you have some practice doing this, you'll be able to tackle more complicated issues. Once you have your upset, answer the following two questions in writing.

1. *What am I upset about?/ Who am I upset with?*
2. *Why?*

Be concise, and use as few words as possible, you're not writing a novel. Fifty words or less. When you feel like you have a clear "what" and "why," move on to the next question. Ask yourself the following question and write down the answer:

3. *What am I making this <u>mean</u> about <u>me</u>?*

The first two questions can be easy enough to answer. The third one can be very tricky and it's pretty much impossible to try and answer this question without your feelings getting in the way of seeing what you're thinking.

When you're looking for what you're making something mean about you, it's connected to the story you tell yourself, not what's actually true. It's the internal voice that tethers you to what you believe deep down inside. Revealing what that voice is saying to you will lead you to the False Core Belief.

This process is not easy to do. False Core Beliefs don't want to be identified and dismantled. They feed off your sadness and anger. They'll squirm and try to trick you because if you see them for what they are, they'll lose power over you. Try not to get frustrated if it takes a while to find what you're looking for. This is where a processing partner comes in very handy. Another person can often see things we can't because they aren't going to be distracted by the emotions that surround your upset. It's easier for them to see the facts.

To help illustrate this process, here's a made-up example of an upset and how I would process it to identify the False Core Belief at the heart of it.

Identification Exercise Example:

I'm mad at my landlord because he's a jerk and he doesn't care enough to make sure that the front entry to my apartment building is secure and someone is stealing packages from the mail area. If he cared about his tenants, he would do something about it.

The first thing to do is identify what's true in the above statement. Writing things down is so important—you get to see clearly what your thinking is and parse out what's fact, what's an emotion, and what's an opinion. False Core Beliefs are really good at hiding behind emotions and opinions. Setting those aside, looking only at the facts, takes away their hiding place. We're pulling the curtain aside, exposing the Wizard of Oz for who he is—a liar.

Here's how I would break this down. The landlord isn't fixing the security problem and packages are being stolen. That's all. The stuff about him being a jerk and not caring is my opinion. They may be *my* truth, but they aren't *the* truth. My neighbors may love my landlord, so to them, he isn't a jerk, therefore it isn't reality, it's my opinion, and right now I'm only looking for what's true about this one problem. If I want to dig into my feelings about my landlord, I can do that later using this same process, but one thing at a time. Truth is hard enough to identify without muddying it up with multiple issues. The only things in that statement that are true are that he isn't fixing the problem and things are being stolen. Once I've identified the truth, and removed my opinions and feelings about it, the statement about my upset now looks like this:

My landlord hasn't fixed the security problem at the entrance to my building and packages are being stolen.

Next, I ask myself focused questions about that statement to reveal the False Core Belief. I'm not digging for evidence to justify my feelings—this is important—I've set those aside for now. This is about what I think, not how I feel. I'm looking for what I'm making the upset mean about me as a human being, which will lead me to my False Core Belief. Now that I have my revised statement, void of feelings and opinions, I dig deeper to reveal the thinking;

My landlord hasn't fixed the security problem in my building and packages are being stolen. What am I making this *mean* about *me*?

It means my packages aren't safe.

True, my packages aren't safe. But that's about the packages, not me. Now, what am I making it mean about me that my packages aren't safe?

What am I making that mean about me? I guess it means that my landlord doesn't care about me.

Okay, I'm getting closer, but I'm still making it about my landlord, not about me. What am I making it mean about me that my packages aren't safe?

I'm scared that someone is going to steal my packages.

Yes, that's a real possibility, but that is about feelings. I'm looking for what I believe to be true, not how I feel about it. So, what does it mean about me if someone steals my packages?

If someone steals my package, I won't get the new stuff I bought.

And if I don't get the new stuff I bought, what does that mean about me?

It means I'm out fifty bucks.

And if I'm out fifty bucks, what does that mean about me?

It means I wasted my money.

And what does it mean about me if I waste money?

It means that I can't manage my money very well.

Okay, hold there. I'm actually very good at managing my money. When I had my reviews at work I was always being praised for my fiscal responsibility and how I'm great at staying on budget. So, telling myself that I can't manage my money very well is absolutely not an empirical truth about me. It's a flag that I'm getting close to something. Now I ask:

What does it mean about me if I can't manage my money very well?

It means I shouldn't be buying nice things for myself.

Getting closer. And what does it mean about me if I shouldn't buy nice things for myself?

It means I don't deserve nice things.

Bingo! There it is, I found it. This incessant False Core Belief comes up for me time and time again. It has kept me from being kind to myself my whole life. Let's see if there's more hiding in there:

And what does it mean about me if I don't deserve nice things?

It means I'll never have nice things.

And what does it mean about me if I'll never have nice things?

It means I'm not good enough to have nice things.

Double whammy. "I don't deserve nice things "and "I'm not good enough" are two of my False Core Beliefs. Closely related but distinct. Now I understand what's under the surface.

I've gone from being really pissed at my landlord, to recognizing that my upset about the packages going missing is more about my False Core Belief that I'm not good enough to deserve the nice thing I ordered online than it is about the security door. I may still be upset about the security door and need to follow up with my landlord, who I may still think is a jerk, but now I can address the security door issue without it being fueled with emotions stemming from my False Core Beliefs. I can contact him about the problem with the door without the False Core Belief driving the conversation. This process makes it possible for me to make choices based on the present moment, not the past. Instead of flying off the handle and yelling at my landlord about the door, which is a *reaction*, I can *choose a response*, to talk calmly about a serious problem that needs to be addressed as soon as possible.

Hopefully, this example has given you enough of a foundation and understanding to take on your own upsets. Once you've processed your first one using this tool, you can make a list of upsets and start going through them in the same fashion to discover your False Core Beliefs. Answer the first two questions for each upset—*what am I upset about, and why*— so you have a clear and concise "what" and "why." You may find yourself getting stuck on the third question—*what am I making this mean about me?*— especially if you're doing the exercise alone. Don't worry about it. A processing partner can be incredibly useful to help steer you in the right direction. Ask for assistance from them if you need it.

Stay with smaller upsets to start. This is not the only list you'll ever make. Just as with physical exercise, you need to build muscle before you can add heavier weight. Don't do heavy emotional lifting until you have a strong foundation. As you practice this exercise, you'll gain insight to identify your own list of False Core Beliefs more easily. You'll get better at it and it'll be easier to take on the larger issues. As you do this, you'll discover more of what's beneath the surface of your upsets and you'll begin to identify your own list of False Core Beliefs.

The problem with False Core Beliefs in general is that they just aren't true. None of them. If you dig down and find that your core belief is, "I'm Awesome," that's not a False Core Belief. You are awesome, that's true! False Core Beliefs aren't positive thoughts. I suggest you dig a little deeper. It's likely that what is underneath "I'm awesome", is something like, "I have to pretend I like myself so no one will see what a loser I am."

Our Core beliefs were formed from the decisions we made about the world around us when we were too young to understand what we were deciding. Positive beliefs aren't the problem, and I hope you discover some on your journey of discovery. This process is about mining for the things that stop us. You can go even further back and find the source of your False Core Belief if you really want to clean the house, but it's not necessary to get the benefit of the process.

If you choose not to use a processing partner to help you with this exercise, you should share your results with them when you're done. It'll give them insights and understanding of the hard work you've done to expose your False Core Beliefs. What you discovered doing this exercise is going to be especially useful to them when they accompany you in the RITE Thinking Process.

What a beautiful gift awareness is because it starts to open up our ability to make a conscious choice about things instead of being at the mercy of automatic reactions to everything all of the time. But awareness can also be painful. Harsh realities aren't fun to look at. Luckily, it's not the end of the process! We have tools we can use to deal with that awareness.

Questions to ask yourself before moving on:

- What am I afraid I'll discover if I look too closely at myself?
- Are there parts of myself I'm not willing to look at?
- What stops me from seeing what's true?

Chapter Four

Acceptance

I grew up in Minnesota, the "Land of Ten Thousand Lakes." As a little girl, whenever I was on a boat I'd peer over the side, down into the murky depths, trying to spot fish. Once, I saw a freakishly large one slowly rise from the bottom. First, I saw a shadow, then a flicker of movement, not sure what it was, and then it rose like a submarine, becoming clearer the closer it got to the surface. I'd always sensed these monster-sized fish were down where I couldn't see them. I tried not to think about them when I swam, but now and then my foot would brush up against one and scare the living crap out of me. Seeing this monstrosity with my own two eyes was proof they existed, I could no longer just pretend they weren't there. There was nothing for me to do but accept the reality of the fact that these fish were swimming in the same water that I was.

It's impossible to find acceptance around a problem if you haven't identified the problem itself, which is why awareness comes first. After you become aware of something, you can move into the process of acceptance. It can be easier to accept good things. But what happens when the things we're confronted with are totally unacceptable? Why would we go through the process of accepting something painful? Because it gives us access to something we often give away when we're little, especially if we experienced trauma: the power of choice. So, let's go back to our handy dandy dictionary. Here's the definition I found for acceptance:

acceptance[22]

noun

1: the quality or state of being accepted or acceptable: His theories have gained widespread acceptance.

2: the act of accepting something or someone: the fact of being accepted: APPROVAL acceptance of responsibility

3: law: an agreeing either expressly or by conduct to the act or offer of another so that a contract is concluded and the parties become legally bound

4a: the act of accepting a time draft or bill of exchange for payment when due according to the specified terms

b: an accepted draft or bill of exchange

None of these definitions get to the heart of what I'm looking for, they don't really resonate. When this happens, I break down the word or look at its synonyms for more clarity. The first part of this word is "accept," so I go to that definition first and I find what I'm looking for under 3c.

accept[23]

verb

1a: to receive (something offered): willingly accept a gift

b: to be able or designed to take or hold (something applied or added): a surface that will not accept ink

2: to give admittance or approval to accept her as one of the group

3a: to endure without protest or reaction: accept poor living conditions

b: to regard as proper, normal, or inevitable an idea that is widely accepted

c: to recognize as true

---

[22] Merriam-Webster.com
[23] Merriam-Webster.com

It can be difficult to accept things we find unacceptable or objectionable. The thing that's so powerful about definition 3c is that it's a straightforward statement that has no emotional qualifiers attached to it. It simply says we recognize something as true. The key here is that it doesn't say that we have to like it. It isn't like being forced to swallow spinach if we don't like the taste, it's about accepting that spinach is full of iron and potassium and all kinds of things that are healthy, no one is telling us that we have to like the way it tastes.

Acceptance isn't always a simple decision, it's not a magic button, it can be a process. Full acceptance of difficult things comes with time and tending. It's important to keep our emotions separate to start. This doesn't mean that our emotions aren't important, in fact, they're vital to the essence of what it means to be human. It means that moving from resistance to acceptance comes in stages and emotions can stop us from seeing what's true.

~ Reality check ~

Acceptance through the healing lens I'm looking through starts by recognizing the reality of a situation as true, nothing else. As soon as we add emotions to it, we're tethering what we're trying to accept to something that is often immovable—how we feel about the thing. Emotions are powerful, and they're rooted in our core beliefs, good or bad. Accepting the harsh truth about something is often experienced as a contradiction to an emotion attached to it, so we avoid acceptance. Holding an emotional attachment rather than accepting an uncomfortable truth is easier because it feels familiar.

Once you've accepted the reality of something, untethered to the emotional attachment of it, you can move into discovering what's underneath—the False Core Belief. The foundation of that belief system we develop throughout our lives that tells us how we should feel about something. Ask yourself, would you live your adult life based on the advice of a seven-year-old child? With the exception of maybe having ice cream for dinner instead of a healthy salad—because ICE CREAM—I don't think I would. I'd rather decide things based on my adult understanding of the world. So, examining our thinking is essential to the process of acceptance.

Our False Core Beliefs aren't going anywhere— unless you have a brain injury that doesn't allow you to access that part of your brain anymore. They're part of our neural network. For me, those pesky beliefs, that I'm not good enough, that I'm stupid, and that I don't deserve nice things, rise to the surface regardless of my rational mind. That's the bad news. The good news is we can create new neural pathways, and over time they can become as powerful, or even more powerful than the original ones. Huzzah! That means change is possible, so keep reading.

Think of acceptance as a scale of options, and as the scale rises so does our defiance of acceptance. Lowest on the scale are things we find easier to accept, like something we can't have that we really want. Moving along the scale ups our resistance, maybe it's a personal loss, like failing at something we worked hard to accomplish. Further on we might have outrage over social justice concerns that are close to our heart. The stakes will get even higher, something that feels big and insurmountable, like political or world issues beyond our control. At the top are things that hit us at the core of who we are, like the death of someone we love. Resistance exists at every level, but it's much easier to accept a canceled flight than the loss of a pet.

Acceptance is a process that can take a long time. I've identified six layers to address before I can consider accepting something that feels unacceptable.

Layers of Acceptance:

- Layer One- *Identify the upset- What do I find unacceptable?*
- Layer Two- *Accept the reality of the situation as true, without emotional attachment, remembering that I don't need to like something to accept it.*
- Layer Three- *Identify what emotions are attached to the situation.*
- Layer Four- *Honor those emotions- My feelings matter.*

- Layer Five- *What idea do I have to let go of to find acceptance?*
- Layer Six- *How can I reframe an idea that is holding me back from acceptance?*

To illustrate what I'm talking about I'll start small, sharing a struggle from my own life that I found unacceptable, and how I came to a place of acceptance.

Example One:

When my kids were little, we had a dog named Whitney, a black lab mix of some sort, who was a stray we rescued from the animal shelter. She was quirky and had strange habits from her days on the street. For instance, she wouldn't just eat her food out of the bowl we set down for her. She would grab a mouthful of kibble and take it down the hallway, spit it out, and then eat it. We figured this was how she learned to survive in a world where bigger dogs might come and take her food or people would chase her away. She would grab the grub and run to a safe spot to consume it. It took her years to realize we weren't going to take her food away from her.

Whitney had one annoying trait. She loved to chew shoes. Not just any shoes, my shoes—that dog chewed every pair of shoes I owned. Sometimes she would gnaw on a shoelace of someone else's shoe, but she got to every single pair of mine. It seemed like no matter how hard I tried to keep my shoes away from her, she would eventually get at them. A closet door would be left open, which happened a lot in my busy family with young kids, and Whitney had a sixth sense about these things. She would sneak into the closet, drag one of my shoes off into a quiet corner and go to town on it.

We didn't have a lot of money back then so I didn't feel like I could afford new shoes, especially if they would just end up as an expensive doggie chew toy. I resigned myself to the fact that my shoes were junk, but I wasn't happy about it. Every time I wanted to dress nicely, I'd slip into a pair of dress shoes with chew marks on the heels.

It was embarrassing and depressing because it was a daily reminder that tapped into my belief that I don't deserve nice things.

The process of acceptance starts with awareness and grows from there.

Layer One- *Identify the upset- What do I find unacceptable?*
All of my shoes have chew marks on them. I don't believe that I deserve nice things and this shoe situation is evidence that it's true. I don't have enough money to go out and buy myself all new shoes. And even if I did spend the money, the dog would eventually chew them up too so what's the point? I guess I just have to be resigned to the fact that all my shoes are chewed on, but every time I put my shoes on, I'm depressed and aggravated.

Layer Two- *Accept the reality of the situation as true, without emotional attachment, remembering that I don't need to like something to accept it.*
I own a dog that destroys my shoes. She is compelled to do this for reasons unknown because she is a dog and I can't ask her. She might never stop this destructive behavior. (Do you see the lack of emotional attachment in this layer?)

Layer Three- *Identify what emotions are attached to the situation.*
Anger—I love my dog, but she really pisses me off when she does this. This is an expensive problem, and I don't have a lot of money to spare. Sadness—I like my shoes and I'm sad they are ruined. And it's depressing because it reinforces my belief that I don't deserve nice things.

Fear—I'm afraid that if I buy new shoes Whitney will eventually get to them, and it'll perpetuate a cycle of upset. It'll make me feel even worse about spending money on something for myself only to have it destroyed, which will then reinforce the idea that I don't deserve nice things. It feels easier to just walk around in crappy shoes.

Layer Four- *Honor those emotions- My feelings matter.*
It's okay for me to be mad that my dog does this. I get to be sad about something of mine being ruined and it doesn't have to mean anything more than I'm just sad or mad. I want to be happy when I put my shoes on and not feel guilty for buying new shoes when we don't have a lot of extra money.

Layer Five- *What idea do I have to let go of to find acceptance?*
I can let go of the idea that I don't deserve nice things. Just because I'm afraid I don't deserve them, or that I should spend money on my kids instead of myself, doesn't make it true. I deserve nice things as much as anyone else does.

Layer Six- *How can I reframe an idea that is holding me back from acceptance?*
Isn't it even more of a tragedy to deprive myself of something I have a right to, like decent shoes, than the tragedy of having a bunch of chewed-up shoes? Buy some new shoes, woman, and teach your kids to close the closet door so she'll stop getting at them. Even better, put them up on a shelf where she can't reach them!

Once I put these pieces together in my mind, I saw that I had a choice about it. I accepted the fact that I had a dog that loved to chew my shoes and I stopped tethering that reality to my old belief that I don't deserve nice things. What began to happen was that I didn't get thoroughly depressed when I put my shoes on, I could just be annoyed instead of devastated about my pretty high heels being a chew toy.

As I said, acceptance is a process, one that can shift daily. I can find myself in a place of ease regarding something one day, only to find myself in total refusal to accept that same truth the next. Sometimes I have to do this process of uncovering the layers repeatedly before I find acceptance.

Example Two:

My mother died of Alzheimer's. That fact I can accept. I can even accept the fact that she's gone—I'm grateful she isn't suffering anymore. What I have a hard time accepting is how she died, the circumstances of the last week, and the final hours of her life.

This happened during the COVID-19 shutdown. My brothers and I had taken her out of the assisted living situation she was in and brought her home to care for her during the summer of 2020 because we knew that if we left her in there, we would likely not see her again.

In the days before she died, my mom's ability to communicate disappeared. She was confused and panicky and in severe pain from a body riddled with debilitating arthritis. We didn't understand what she wanted because she didn't have the words to tell us, and she didn't understand what we were trying to do to help her.

The last day she was conscious, she fell out of the hospital bed that had been brought in by the at-home hospice team that morning. She had been a handful the entire day, and my brother and I were exhausted. We had been administering the prescribed pain medications and sedatives to calm her throughout the day, which didn't do much to help the situation. We finally got her into bed for the night and were settling in for some rest ourselves when we heard her scream and then a heavy thud. We sprinted into her room and found her unconscious on the floor, her feet tangled in the blanket, and diarrhea covering her back from neck to knee. We assume she was trying to get out of bed and get herself to the bathroom, something she had been unable to do on her own for days, and fell in her effort. She hadn't asked for help because she had no ability to communicate what she needed.

We cleaned her up and lifted her into bed. As we did this she called out. Was this a reaction of surprise? Was it pain? Was it confusion? It's impossible to know. She never spoke again.

The following days were a constant rotation of family members administering her medication with a dropper into her mouth every fifteen minutes because she couldn't swallow much at a time. Every day the nurses would come for their daily check-in and say Mom would be gone, "Any time now," but the next day Mom would still be there. The nurses told us to call if we needed anything, but they were on rounds throughout the city. Because of the pandemic, they were very busy.

We sat with mom, watching and waiting for her to take her final breaths. I lost count of the number of times we thought she was gone only to have her strong heart roar back to life, and the warmth would return to her feet and hands. It was an emotional rollercoaster that seemingly had no end.

And every day we had to change her diaper. When we did this, she would call out. She had been in so much pain the last six months of her life and we didn't want to move her, but we couldn't let her sit in a wet diaper. This went on for eight days.

We considered trying to find a bed for her in a hospice unit or hospital but she was so close to gone we didn't want her dying in an ambulance alone. Because of the COVID restrictions, we would not have been able to be with her in any of those settings, and we didn't want that. And there were so few beds available because of the pandemic so we continued to care for her at home.

The last morning she was with us, I woke up with a start. A thought entered my mind and I feared it was true. We had mom on so much morphine she shouldn't have been so uncomfortable when we moved her. I went to my brothers with my concern. "I think mom broke something in her pelvis when she fell out of bed last week," I said.

When I spoke my concern out loud, it felt less like a worry and more like a fact. The next time we changed her I looked for any bruising or discoloration that might signal a deep bone break, and sure enough I found some. My heart sank. No wonder she was in so much pain. I kicked myself for not figuring it out sooner.

We moved her as little as possible that day with this new awareness. It was another emotional roller coaster of a day, and by dinner time her breathing had changed dramatically. Then a rattling sound that was different from what we had been hearing—her lungs were filling up. When her mouth started to fill with thick mucus, I did my best to keep her mouth clean and we called the hospice hotline. They said they would send someone as soon as possible, but it would be a while before anyone could get there. I talked to her, sang to her, and encouraged her to let go as she was being consumed by the unabating tide of mucus in her mouth.

Over the next hour, we witnessed our mother suffocate to death. By the time the hospice nurse arrived, she was gone. It was brutal. I had nightmares about her death for months. I couldn't get the image out of my head, of my mother gasping for her last breaths and the fear in her eyes, which she had opened in the last minutes of her life. Her death should not have happened that way.

My sadness and anger around these events are palpable. How do you accept something like this? Exploring the layers of this will help illustrate how I've been able to come to a place of acceptance. It's not total, there are days I still struggle with it, but I'm no longer haunted by it.

Layer One- *Identify the upset- What do I find unacceptable?*
Where do I begin? How many synonyms of "angry" do I need to come up with? There are so many things I find unacceptable about this. I'll start with the pandemic and how stretched our healthcare providers had been. Had there not been so much death happening around us because of COVID-19 maybe there would have been more help available to us. Maybe someone who knew what they were doing could have been in the room to make it easier on her.

Next, I'm angry that Alzheimer's took away my mother's ability to communicate and her suffering was increased because she couldn't tell us what was going on.

I'm angry at myself for not putting the pieces of her situation together sooner to ease her amplified suffering.

I'm infuriated that we have to put our loved ones through the torture of dying like she did instead of allowing them a dignified death. There was no way my mother was going to survive. She should have been allowed the option to die on her own terms.

I'm livid that my brothers and I had to witness such a traumatic event, that the last minutes of our time with her were torturous for everyone in the room. I'm apoplectic, knowing it didn't have to be that way. If I give up my anger it feels like I'm *giving up*, like the unacceptable death wins.

Layer Two- *Accept the reality of the situation as true, without emotional attachment, remembering that I don't need to like something to accept it.*
This is very hard to do because my emotions are so strong. I don't want to let go of my anger because I feel like I have the right to be angry. But continuing to see this through the lens of my anger is only going to perpetuate the feeling. If I want to find acceptance, I need to set my emotions aside, for the moment, knowing I'll come back to them. So, I look to see what's true, what is the reality of the situation, not how I feel about it.

The reality is my mother died a painful death. I chose to be there, to witness it because I didn't want her to be alone. A global health crisis prevented us as a family from being able to provide proper support for her in her final hour. The way a person dies is not up to them, and the timing of what happens can't always be controlled. The body does what the body does. Disease is a part of life, the nature of living this human existence. The ways in which the body can cease to function as intended are limitless and often beyond our control. Science and medicine can only do so much. Death is inevitable.

Layer Three- *Identify what emotions are attached to the situation.*
I'm every shade of angry and I believe I have the right to stay angry. I fear that letting go of my anger will mean that I'm okay with how she died, and I'm not. I don't think I ever will be. Truth be told, I don't ever want to *not* be angry about it because I think my anger is justified. My feelings of guilt and sadness around not putting the pieces together sooner are hard to let go of because I feel like she suffered more because of me. I want to beat myself up for causing her more pain.

Layer Four- *Honor those emotions- My feelings matter.*
I do have the right to be angry, it was totally messed up and unfair. I don't need to force myself to feel anything other than what I feel. I'm pissed. And sad for her. And sad for me and my brothers. It was horrible to witness, and I wish so desperately that it didn't happen that way.

Layer Five- *What idea do I have to let go of to find acceptance?*
My guilt and sadness around not figuring out what happened sooner are attached to my unrealistic personal demand of perfection, tied to my belief that I have to do everything right. I'm not a doctor or a nurse, and they didn't figure it out either. My expectation of perfection, especially in a situation like this, is unrealistic and I set myself up for failure if that is what I'm going to demand of myself. I didn't do anything wrong. I stayed with her and did the best I could under the circumstances, and I know she appreciated my being there. I can let go of the idea that I'm responsible for her pain. In fact, my presence probably made the whole situation less painful for her, not more.

As for my anger, I need to let go of the idea that acceptance means I'm okay with how it happened, or that my anger is no longer justified if I give in to acceptance. What I'm doing is allowing acceptance to co-exist with my anger. And I need to honor my feelings. What I don't need to do is *give over* to my anger. It does not need to be the driving force of this experience.

Layer Six- *How can I reframe an idea that is holding me back from acceptance?*
Again, this is very challenging because it's so close to my heart. So, I take a deep breath and look at what I think I can do right now. This will be an evolution.

The main idea that is holding me back is feeling like the situation, my mother's horrible death, will win if I accept it. But there are no winners and losers here. It feels like there is because of the loss of my mother. Can I reframe the idea, and change the story? What if I'm the winner? What if I consider the fact that we were able to keep our mother at home and she didn't die alone as a win? It's really important. We accomplished something that mattered to us and to her. I can actually celebrate that.

I can let go of the idea that I didn't do it perfectly in my eyes, I can embrace my humanity and forgive myself for not seeing something that no one else saw either. I can thank my brain for doing some hard work while I slept so I had some clarity when I woke up, and her last day was less painful than the days preceding it. That was a gift.

All of this makes me feel a little better. It doesn't take it away, but it establishes a new neuropathway for my thoughts to travel instead of the one it was on. I'll need to keep reminding myself of these things as time goes by. The evolution of grieving can be slow. There are things that will happen, thoughts that will enter my mind that want to pull me back to my righteous anger. It's my job to be aware of my thoughts and honor the emotions when they come up so I can move through them and not get stuck in them.

Example Three:

I'm a survivor of multiple experiences of sexual violence. In my memoir, I talk about the four events that happened to me between the ages of ten and nineteen. These experiences shaped me, and not in a good way. I suffered from years of unaddressed PTSD in part because I wasn't ready to look at what happened and how I'd been affected.

As part of the discovery stage for the lawsuit I filed in 2015, I was required to talk to a psychiatrist about my past, to reveal everything and anything I could remember about my life no matter how relevant I thought it was. I told her everything I could think of, including the four incidents of sexual violence before I turned twenty, and how I didn't fight off my assailants, how my fear response in every assault was to freeze while I was being assaulted.

I also told her about an experience I had in my early twenties, a story I didn't include in my memoir but will share here to illustrate how deeply denial can go.

I'd been vacationing in Mexico with my boyfriend and another couple. We were hanging out on the beach, like you do in Mexico, and two young Mexican local guys showed up and hung out with us. Their English was limited but they seemed fun and very interested in us.

We decided to do a very touristy thing and went out on a boat to be towed around the bay on a thing called an Island Hopper, commonly referred to as a banana boat. I was interested in riding it, but our traveling companions didn't have any interest in going out on the water, and my boyfriend just wanted to go on the boat, so we invited our new friends to come along.

My boyfriend got on the boat and I got on the hopper with the two local guys. Somehow, I ended up sandwiched between the two of them. The boat started up and away we went. It was exhilarating and fun—for about thirty seconds.

I was holding onto the guy in front of me with both arms because we were going very fast. I was wearing a bikini bathing suit and the guy sitting behind me suddenly reached his hand inside my bikini bottoms and shoved his fingers deep inside my vagina. I immediately overturned the hopper by leaning all the way over to the left towards the water rushing past my face and we plunged into the water with this guy's hand still inside me. The force of the water as we fell off the hooper was what physically broke us apart. As I tumbled around under the surface of the water, I was so grateful to be off that stupid thing, and when I came to the surface, I turned to the guy who had assaulted me, pointed my finger at his face, and said the only word I knew he would understand, "No!"

I began to swim frantically away from them. My boyfriend was calling to me from the boat to climb in, but I was in flight mode, and so upset I didn't want to be anywhere near those two creeps, so without a word of explanation I just swam. We had made it pretty far out from shore in the short but fast ride on the hopper, and I was definitely struggling after several minutes of swimming hard, but I'd rather have drowned than get in that boat. I don't say that to be dramatic; I truly would rather have died.

When I got to the sand, my boyfriend, who had ridden to shore on the boat, ran up the beach to me and asked me what happened, and why I wouldn't get in the boat. When I told him the guy behind me had put his hand in my bathing suit, my boyfriend immediately turned to go find the two creeps, but they'd both disappeared off the beach. We never saw them again.

At the time, I didn't fully understand what was going on with me, why I hadn't been more levelheaded, gotten on the boat, and told my boyfriend about the assault right then and there. I now understand that my amygdala was fully engaged and in charge, and my instinct was to flee. My prefrontal cortex was offline and I was in complete primal mode.

I never forgot that this event happened, I just didn't allow myself to be fully present to the memory of it. That is until a few years ago when I stumbled across a bunch of photos from that trip and saw a picture I'd taken of these two creeps hanging out on the beach with us before I was assaulted. I finally understood the depth of how I was affected by what I experienced that day.

I held the picture in my hand and it started to shake. I was transported back to that moment. My heart rate went soaring, I felt dizzy and panicky. It was just a picture, but my body didn't see it that way. The picture was representative of a rape. Another rape. A fifth rape. For those who are wondering how a guy sticking his hand in your bathing suit is defined as a "rape," here's the definition:

rape [24]
: *unlawful sexual intercourse or any other sexual penetration of the vagina, anus, or mouth of another person, with or without force, by a sex organ, other body part, or foreign object, without the consent of the victim.*

Even though I'd told the psychiatrist about it during that interview, I didn't consciously include it in my mental list of sexual vio-

---

[24] Dictionary.com

lence episodes. I chose to only write about the four earlier events in my memoir. I didn't want to include this violation with the other events because it was so idiotic of me to climb on that contraption. I'm embarrassed to even admit it happened. In order for me to find acceptance around this embarrassing and traumatic event, I need to look at it. Okay, deep breath—here we go.

Layer One- *Identify the upset- What do I find unacceptable?*
I'll start with the obvious part of the story that's upsetting—I was violated physically. That in and of itself is enough to be upset about. Then there's the fact that I chose to get on that banana boat in the first place without even considering that I might be sexually assaulted while riding it. What an idiot I was. You'd think I'd know better, that my "Spidey-senses" would have been going wacky. But no, this naïve dingbat, me, blindly walked into a situation where I was wearing a bikini bathing suit, spread my legs wide to straddle this giant floating phallic symbol, tucked myself snuggly in between two guys I didn't know from Adam, and I didn't think twice about it. I'm not sure I've ever done anything more stupid.

Layer Two- *Accept the reality of the situation as true, without emotional attachment, remembering that I don't need to like something to accept it.*
This is really hard to do because my brain is screaming at me, "Yup, that was incredibly stupid." But here goes— I was raped in public.

Hmmmm. Shouldn't there be more? I want to attach a bunch of qualifiers to this one, to present evidence of my stupidity. But this really is it, it's simple—I was a victim of sexual assault. I was raped in public.

Layer Three- *Identify what emotions are attached to the situation.*
I'm still kind of soaking in the reality of that, absent of the story I've been telling myself all along. Wow.

Okay, looking now at the emotional attachment. I don't want to let go of this internal monologue that I'm at fault, that I'm an idiot.

I can identify a powerful positive-negative (more on that in the next chapter). If I hold onto that narrative, I get to be right about the belief that I'm stupid. Also, I'm afraid. If, after all I'd been through, I still didn't see something harmful coming at me, I must be broken beyond repair. A broken compass that can't find North. I'm also really sad—statistics show that once a girl is sexually assaulted, she is more likely to have it happen again—in my case, again, and again, and again, and again. It's deeply tragic, not just for me, but for all women. Oh, and one more thing—I'm mad as hell.

Layer Four- *Honor those emotions- My feelings matter.*
I don't like to allow myself to be angry about how women are treated in the world because the realities are so overwhelmingly prevalent if I do let myself get angry, I'll be mad 24/7. Our basic rights aren't a given, even in the "most advanced" country on the planet.

I'm going to refrain from conflating all of the injustices women have to endure and attaching them to this story—though it would take no effort whatsoever to connect those dots. Instead, I'll stay with the feelings around this specific event.

It angers me to no end that a guy on a beach could think he has the right to shove his fingers inside a woman without consent. But this is the reality of the world we live in.

This is a sad thing that happened to me, and I get to feel sad, and fragile, and hurt, and angry, and betrayed, and stupid, and confused, and like I want to disappear, and whatever else might show up around this event because it's *my experience*. It's how I feel and my feelings matter. I get to feel them and not allow shame to rob me of the natural cycle of being impacted by something, feeling the emotions around it, then moving through them and letting it go. I don't need to keep myself trapped mid-cycle.

Here's the one thing I can hold onto that makes me proud of myself—I didn't freeze. I may have been naïve enough to get on that stupid banana boat in the first place, but I had a physical reaction different from the past. In every other sexual assault I'd experienced,

I froze. But not this time. I fought and got out of there. So yeah, I get to feel proud of myself for that.

Layer Five- *What idea do I have to let go of to find acceptance?*

I've felt broken beyond repair since I was a little girl. I had childhood ailments that gave me some pretty solid proof that there was something truly wrong with me. The beliefs established during that time burrowed down into my psyche and have endured. Feeling like I'm broken and stupid is as natural for me as breathing.

I need to be willing to let myself off the hook. To stop blaming myself for someone else's actions. I need to let go of the proof of my naiveté, my stupidity.

Layer Six- *How can I reframe an idea that is holding me back from acceptance?*

Just because I didn't see something coming doesn't mean I'm stupid. It's actually a good thing that I'm willing to be vulnerable and want to trust people. It allows me to have deep meaningful relationships.

I was barely an adult when this happened, and my experiences as a teenager in an environment where the sexualization of children was normalized didn't exactly set me up for knowing how to trust my instincts. I was trained to ignore them, so it makes sense that I wouldn't see this coming.

Once I have a handle on what is keeping me from accepting things I find difficult, if I can allow the idea of acceptance to sit calmly in my heart and not have it bouncing off the walls, I can take a step towards action.

Questions to ask yourself before moving on:

- What are the things in my life that I find unacceptable?
- What am I afraid I'll have to give up if I accept something I don't want to accept?
- Am I ready to momentarily set aside my emotions in order to see what's true?

Chapter Five

Action

When everything aligns and I find a moment of perfection, I swim in the sweetness of the sense of ease that comes with it. When the tone rings true, I can just sit back and listen, knowing there's nothing else I need to do. But when I find myself making missteps, realizing I made mistakes that affect my life or others in negative ways—feeling like I'm falling into an abyss of self-doubt and loathing, or recognize there's something I resist accepting—I can use the 3 A's to bring myself back to center again. To see what's true about a situation so I can make informed choices about what to do next.

By now it should be clear that a lack of awareness and acceptance will keep you from being in action, but before I take the deep dive into what action looks like, it's important to look at the things that stop us from being in action, and the biggest one is fear.

~ Fear ~

I can't tell you how many times I haven't done something because of this stupid four-letter word. Don't get me wrong, fear is an important emotion and can keep us safe. But if it's running the show, it can also be the ultimate set of handcuffs. Fear of [fill in the blank] will squash the best-laid plans, the wildest dreams. Fear of failure, fear of success, fear of doing a fantastic job that goes unnoticed. There are a million forms of fear.

I've heard it said that the opposite of fear isn't trust, it's love. Deep inside, this rings true for me. But how could "love" combat my fear of seeing someone in public that causes me to have a panic attack? Maybe I'm not in a place where I want to be loving to that person.

Love doesn't seem like the right tool to combat that particular fear, so I'll start with the word "fear" as a verb since we're talking about action.

fear[25]
verb
1: to be afraid of: expect with alarm, fear the worst
2: to have a reverential awe or fear of God
3 archaic: FRIGHTEN
4 archaic: to feel fear in (oneself)

It seems like I need to dig deeper because none of these are shining further light for me. The word that feels like the right one to follow is "Frighten" in the archaic definition 3.

frighten
verb
1: to make afraid: TERRIFY: The movie scene frightened the child.
2: to drive or force by frightening: frightened the boy into confessing

"To drive by force." There it is, in definition 2. Fear is a destructive force. It has power over me at a primal level. The amygdala is the part of the brain that controls fight, flight, freeze, or fawn. It's hard to resist its power. If the opposite of fear is love, how can that release me from fear? I think of love as an emotion, and I know that emotions aren't always the best guide when it comes to truth. My feelings can deceive me. Love is blind, and can make me do stupid things, so how is it going to save me? Let's look at "love" as a verb too.

---

[25] All definitions in this section are from Merriam-Webster.com

love
verb
1: to hold dear: CHERISH
2a: to feel a lover's passion, devotion, or tenderness for
　　(1): CARESS
　　(2): to fondle amorously
　　(3): to copulate with
3: to like or desire actively: take pleasure in: loved to play the violin
4: to thrive in: the rose loves sunlight

I'll steer clear of the aspects of fondling and copulating, that's a different book entirely. I'll focus on the first definition. "To hold dear: Cherish" I'm struck by the word cherish, and not just because it's in all caps, it feels like it's pointing me to something that might be useful, so I go to that definition and see this:

cherish
verb
1a: to hold dear: feel or show affection for: cherished her friends
b: to keep or cultivate with care and affection: NURTURE: cherishes his marriage
2: to entertain or harbor in the mind deeply and resolutely: still cherishes that memory

"Cultivate" in 1b is getting closer, it feels like a tool, whereas "hold dear" feels like a soft puppy that makes me want to cry. Cultivate is a word that is loving but not wimpy, I can feel the motion in this word, so I go there:

cultivate
transitive verb
1: to prepare, or prepare and use, for the raising of crops. Some fields are cultivated while others lie fallow. also: to loosen or break up the soil about growing plants

2a: to foster the growth of, cultivate vegetables cultivate coffee
b: CULTURE SENSE 2Acultivate oysters for pearls
c: to improve by labor, care, or study: REFINE cultivate the
mind... cultivated a reputation as a hard-core wheeler-dealer
3: FURTHER, ENCOURAGE cultivate the arts
4: to seek the society of: make friends with looking for influen-
tial people to cultivate as friends

I love the image of loosening or breaking up soil in the first definition of "Cultivate." And "foster the growth of" in 2a has such a
quiet strength. I feel like I have arrived at an understanding of this
aspect of love that makes sense to me in the context of using it as a
counterbalance to fear.

Love in the face of fear is a gentle strength, a constant that allows
for something to be cultivated or fostered. It's not a big slobbery dog
licking your face, forcing you to be distracted from your fear. It's light
steady rain that makes the hard soil that your fear lives in malleable.
That love may be directed outward, if it's safe to do so, or love can be
directed inward, as compassion for self. Embracing your humanity,
and recognizing that life is messy and that you'll make mistakes, will
fortify your courage and create the possibility of cultivating something different.

Just as acceptance can be a slow evolution, so too can be the
transition from fear into action. There are even times when fear will
not subside. But you don't have to be without fear to be in action.
And I'm not talking about being fearless, I'm talking about courage.
There's a big difference. I can get paralyzed by my fears, but when
I take my fear by the hand and stay in motion anyway, that's when
amazing things happen. Courage is the stuff of survivors, those who
walk forward, not knowing how it'll turn out but doing it anyway
because it's the next right thing to do.

Courage has many faces. I see it in children, stretching themselves
to reach a handlebar that's just out of reach. I see it in teenagers asking someone they like to go to the prom knowing that person might
say no. I see it in protesters standing up for what they believe in,

knowing they might be arrested. I see it in victims of sexual violence breaking their silence and calling out their abusers. These actions are all born of courage and aren't bound by fear.

~ Perfectionism ~

Another form of courage is being willing to make mistakes. As a child actor at the Children's Theatre Company, the expectations were incredibly high. Children and adults were held to the same standard, and I learned quickly that the consequence of mistakes was often ridicule and humiliation.

This kind of conditioning is how my healthy trait, a desire to strive for perfection, got blown out of proportion and became over-sized. Mistakes, even small ones, felt unacceptable. The want for perfection became a need, which makes me either obsessed with perfection to the point I'll burn myself out with the need for it, or feeling defeated and incompetent to the point of being paralyzed if I can't acquire it.

I went back to school in my thirties. I was taking a computer class, something I was most definitely not good at. I was having a complete meltdown one day and I told a friend that I was terrified to go to this class. It was required for my degree, so I couldn't avoid it. She asked me why I was so scared and I confessed that I didn't know anything about what I'd be studying and I was afraid of looking stupid. My friend gently said to me, "Laura, it's called 'school' for a reason. You aren't *supposed* to know everything. You're there to *learn*." This may seem ridiculous to some of you, but it was very real to me.

As I've said, I believe deep down that I'm stupid, so going into a classroom with no knowledge of the subject was incredibly uncomfortable for me. If I didn't already know everything, everyone would see that my belief that I'm stupid is *true*. But my friend's words allowed me to let go of that belief and see what was true: I was there to learn. In fact, I was paying good money to be taught how to do something. What a notion—I'm not going to be chastised for not knowing something. I became aware that my belief system was holding me back, I accepted the reality that I don't have to know everything to show up and learn, and I was able to go into the class, stumble around for a few days, and eventually ace the class.

Now that I'm aware of how my relationship to perfectionism has affected me, and I can see how out of proportion it is, my desire for self-acceptance comes to the surface. I accept the reality that I'm not perfect, and that perfection is healthy as an ideal but not necessarily as an unfailing standard. I fully embrace my messy humanness. This helps me reject the knee-jerk reaction to berate and belittle myself, or not try at all because failure is unacceptable. I have a choice. *I can choose a response and not just react.* I give myself permission to try things and fail, like a normal human being. I can now take action where there previously was none, or choose no action where in the past I felt compelled to drive myself until my tank was empty. Sometimes the right action is no action.

I held such a high standard for myself for the majority of my life. My assistants at work had to endure my charging in and taking things over from them in mid-stroke, so that the reflection of imperfection wouldn't find footing in my department. Good lord, how horrible for them. Thankfully, I was able to let go of some of that in the last years running that department.

Yours Truly has put my size-ten foot in my mouth more times than I care to admit. I've said the wrong thing, pressed send on an email before thinking about it, and not followed an impulse I should have listened to. And there are times when I fail miserably. Oh Lordy, how I can botch it. I can do things that feel in line with my well-being, only to set someone else off balance or knock them over because of my attempt at self-care. I try to do my best, to stay in line with my truth and do no harm. I'm not always successful. But for someone who has suffered from epic levels of self-deprecation, I can now say that I accept my humanness and find comfort in knowing that I won't always do things right. It frees me from crippling perfectionism. I'm done with beating myself up for being human. I fully accept that I'm perfectly imperfect.

~ The Positive-Negative ~

The positive-negative is a crafty little bugger that can prevent me from seeing what's true and being in action. It's attached to a need many of us have—the need to be right. I don't like to be wrong; it makes me cranky. Being right gives me a sense of comfort, even if being right means I'm right about something that isn't a good or healthy thing. It's a positive reinforcement of a negative thought or belief— a positive-negative. Wrong equals powerless. Right equals powerful. I don't know about you, but I prefer the feeling of being powerful over powerless, so leaning into the positive-negative feels comfortable.

We need to get our False Core Beliefs out of the way to accept the reality of something so we can move on. Acceptance is about truth, and False Core Beliefs are about *untruth*. When something happens that provides support to a False Core Belief, it can show up as proof-positive that the belief is true. It supports the lies we tell ourselves and keeps us from seeing the truth, therefore acceptance can evade us.

Looking more closely at my reaction to Whitney chewing my shoes, I see how it triggered my False Core Belief that I don't deserve nice things. I also recognize that one of the reasons I didn't do anything about it for so long wasn't only because the False Core Belief was engaged, but I also got to be right about not deserving nice things if I held onto the chewed shoes. It kept me from throwing them out and buying something to keep my shoes safe from the dog. Deep down, I didn't believe I deserved to spend that much money on myself. Buying new shoes would debunk that, and show I was wrong about not deserving nice things. The shoes were evidence, proof of my False Core Belief, and keeping them allowed me to be *right*. And Right = Powerful.

When I was assaulted on the banana boat, my False Core Beliefs that "I'm stupid" and "broken beyond repair" were reinforced. Blocking myself from being present to the reality of what happened, choosing to not look closely at that event for so long, allowed that memory to sit and fester in the darkness of my mind, whispering to me for decades that I'm an idiot for getting myself into that situation. Proof-positive that I'm about as stupid as they come. I may not be happy about it, but at least I get to be right!

Still not getting it? Try thinking about it as a math equation: X (proof-positive) = Y (I get to be right). Positive-negatives are powerful, and one way to expose these crafty saboteurs is to ask yourself this question when you're struggling to let go of something: would I rather be right, or would I rather be happy?

~ Time to Get Moving ~

I've spent much of my life putting the needs of others ahead of my own at the cost of my physical, mental, and emotional well-being. Over recent years I've learned how to honor my own needs. But there are times when it's important to set aside our needs, to do something for a single person, or the greater good, making sacrifices because it's the right thing to do. Recognizing when it's time to stand up for what feels right for ourselves and when to let go can be extremely difficult. Balance is key.

Your very existence is proof you have what it takes to do something hard. You've worked emotional muscles that allowed you to cope—you have the ability to survive. You can take that ability and apply it to a new set of muscles, ones that allow you to experience the best parts of what it is to be a human being. You're strong enough to learn a different way to take care of yourself.

The circumstances of your life have led you here. If you're waiting for the perfect moment to start this journey of being in action, there's no better time than now. There may be a part of you that wants to run in the other direction and not look back. The wounded part of you doesn't want to be known. Like a sick animal, comfortable hiding in the shadows, festering in the stillness, it lurks there because it knows that if you see it for what it is, it'll lose power over you. Your discomfort is its nirvana. It wants no place in the light of day and scurries away like a cockroach when the light switch flips on, and it wants to drag you into the shadows with it. Resist! That pain is not in charge of your life—you are.

There are people around you who might not want you to change, to be strong. They may think they do, but once you find your footing it can alter your shape and size because you'll no longer be limited by shame and fear. That might scare them. They may have to adjust, maybe even look closely at themselves. They may not be ready to do that because change can be scary. But don't fear your strength. Embrace it.

In this book, you may find a new set of instruments to play or a different way to play the ones you already have. New sounds will come out of you, and it will change you and the world around you. The beauty of it will soar overhead and fill the air. Some people won't be able to hear it over the winds of distraction, of a culture that wants to continue the status quo, but others will hear it. And they'll be inspired by your song. Sing it—loudly.

When I freed myself of old patterns, when I was no longer carrying the weight of the way things were, when the pressures that didn't serve my wellness dissipated, I was able to walk boldly towards a light that was brighter than anything I'd ever known— the light of truth. I sincerely hope you find this too. And when you do, you can breathe deeply, and rest. But right now, it's time to be in action!

Questions to ask yourself before moving on:

- What stops me from being in action?
- Would I rather be right or happy?
- Am I ready to walk forward despite my fear?

Chapter Six

The RITE Thinking Process

rite[26]

noun

1: a prescribed form or manner governing the words or actions for a ceremony

The RITE Thinking Process[27] is a way to address False Core Beliefs. It's something I've been doing for a long time, a distillation of many different techniques I've learned from, and then combined in a "take what you like and leave the rest" kind of way. When I was thinking about what I'd name this thing I do, I decided on RITE as a good acronym. A "rite" is a kind of ceremony, and I like a word that points to the importance of processing in this way, that it has more weight to it than something like journaling.

I'm not trying to reinvent the wheel here. People have been teaching these things and writing books about self-help for longer than I've been alive. And honestly, there might not be anything new in what you read here, but if you're anything like me, sometimes it takes hearing something several times, or in a new way, for it to sink in. This is a way I use to make sense of the thoughts that tumble around in my brain, (or spin out of control depending on the day) and I offer it to you.

Now that you understand the concepts around the 3 A's, have identified some False Core Beliefs, and looked at fear, love, courage,

---

[26] Merriam-Webster.com

[27] Special thanks to Roger Bruner, Mildred Frank, and Ellie Hyatt for passing on their wisdom to me. What I learned from them is the bedrock of the RITE Thinking Process.

and perfectionism, it's time to see what this has all been leading to. I'd say it's the ultimate form of being in action to transform negative thinking. The four stages of the RITE Thinking Process are:

- R- Recognize the thought: Write it out. Expose the thinking. Be concise.
- I- Identify the False Core Belief: See what's underneath the thought.
- T- Tell yourself the truth: Turn it around. Say what's true.
- E- Engage with a response. Don't just sit there, make a decision and do it.

Stage One- *Recognize the thought*
This is similar to the first question in the Identifying False Core Beliefs exercise. Sometimes it's hard to identify what you're thinking because emotions are strong. It might take a conversation with someone to reveal the thinking.

Stage Two- *Identify the False Core Belief*
Go to the list you created while identifying your False Core Beliefs. You should be able to find it on the list, or a variation on one of them. You might even find a new one.

Stage Three- *Tell yourself the truth*
This is hard to do on your own at first, in a similar way that identifying your False Core Beliefs is. Seeing what's true often requires an outside voice, ask your processing partner for help. A simple rule for stage three is to read the thought and look to the opposite of that thought to turn it around. Easier said than done. It's not always obvious, so it can take some time.

Stage Four- *Engage with a response*
Newton's third law is: *For every action, there is an equal and opposite reaction.* That's physics, it makes sense if you understand the science of it. But this law does not and should not apply to our emotional

landscape. You want to move away from reacting, and toward making a choice. Human relations are nuanced, and there's no steadfast rule like Newton's third law that can guide us here.

Most of us go through life reacting to the world around us, bumping up against the circumstances that happen to us, or the world around us, like a ball in a pinball machine. We have little to no ability to do much else because we're at the mercy of our False Core Beliefs that paralyze our decision-making process. Identifying those misconceptions and seeing them for what they are—decisions we made based on false information—gives us the freedom to choose, to *engage with a response* instead of simply reacting.

~ My Processing Example ~

To give you examples of what these stages look like together, I'm going to share one of my own lists of negative thoughts that I processed using RITE Thinking. It's personal and extremely detailed to illustrate a wide variety of my negative thoughts and how I processed them. I didn't hold back any of my negative thoughts— in fact, the list was even longer than this, I've pared it down for the sake of brevity. The point is, it's important to expose all of your thinking. You do yourself a disservice if you if you aren't willing to look in all the corners of your mind.

I was writing my memoir at the time I made this list and was digging into some very painful memories. I wrote it on April 25, 2020, a few weeks after COVID-19 shut down the United States. It was a terrifying time, and my thinking was going into scary places, so I got on my computer and wrote down, as concisely as possible, all of the things that were bothering me, my feelings, and anything negative that came up. It's a pretty sad list—it was a bad day.

Just so you know, you do <u>not</u> need to tackle this much processing in one sitting if you decide to give this a go. In fact, don't! Pick one thought at a time. If you get through one of your own and feel like you're gaining understanding, do another. And give yourself permission to walk away from it too. It can take a lot of time to grasp this, so don't beat yourself up if it doesn't come easily. This is really hard. Because I'm an overachiever, I would look at this list and think I needed to match its length or do even more. If that's what happens to you, or you feel intimidated by the volume, let that go. I'm sharing this with you because it gives you lots of examples, not to set the bar of an achievement standard. For some, this list and the examples of processing may feel tedious, even redundant. In fact, it is. But it is also deeply nuanced, and I want to display a wide variety in hope that everyone reading may find something they can relate to. Bear with me.

Stage One- Recognize the Thought

- I'm agitated, have no motivation, and feel like a fraud. Why would anyone want to read a book that I write?
- I have nothing to contribute that would be useful.
- I think I'm more intelligent than I am.
- I've "snowed" a lot of people into believing that I have something valuable to contribute because I'm an actor, I can talk a good talk.
- Theater as a field is going to die because of COVID-19, and if it doesn't why would anyone even bother hiring me?
- My greatest passion as a performer, singing, is long past. My voice is shot. I can't project anymore without pain.
- People don't really like me, they tolerate me. Once they know me, they don't stick around.
- I'm a pain in the ass, I do things wrong all the time and no one will want to spend energy trying to have a healthy relationship with me because I can't do it right. I f**k things up.
- My old cat is driving me nuts. He won't eat but is always hungry and asking for food. He climbs on everything I'm doing and knocks stuff to the ground, and I'm really tired of it. I feel like things would be better if he weren't here, then I feel like a horrible person for thinking that.

- Grace won't return my emails or texts. I've worn out my welcome with her. She probably wishes she didn't get involved with me regarding the nonprofit. I'm more trouble than I'm worth.
- Anyone who thinks I have value is stupid.
- I will spend the rest of my life alone.
- I'm a worthless piece of crap.
- I want to break something.
- I look old and fat.
- I'm so lonely.
- I can't do anything right.
- I'm too much work.

Ugh, hard to let that soak in. I'm pretty sure every single one of my False Core Beliefs were triggered that day. Let's look at Stage Two and see if I'm right. I'm going to go back to each item on my very sad list to see what story I'm telling myself inside my head. Sometimes more than one False Core Belief is engaged in a single thought. Here's my personal False Core Belief list again for quick reference:

- **I'm broken and I can't be fixed**
- **I don't deserve _____ [fill in the blank]**
- **My needs are less important than the needs of others**
- **I'm not _____ enough [fill in the blank]**
- **If people really knew me, they would go away**
- **I'm stupid**

Now let's see how they showed up: **False Core Beliefs are in bold writing.**

Stage Two- Identify the False Core Belief

- I'm agitated, have no motivation, and feel like a fraud. Why would anyone want to read a book that I write? **I'm not _ good_ enough**

- I have nothing to contribute that would be useful. **I'm not _smart_ enough**
- I think I'm more intelligent than I am. **I'm stupid**
- I've "snowed" a lot of people into believing that I have something valuable to contribute because I'm an actor, I can talk a good talk. **If people really knew me, they would go away**
- Theater as a field is going to die because of COVID-19, and if it doesn't why would anyone even bother hiring me? **I don't deserve _a career in theater_** and **If people really knew me, they would go away**
- My greatest passion as a performer, singing, is long past. My voice is shot. I can't project anymore without pain. **I'm broken and I can't be fixed**
- People don't really like me, they tolerate me. Once they know me, they don't stick around. **If people really knew me, they would go away** and **I don't deserve _good friends_**
- I'm a pain in the ass, I do things wrong all the time and no one will want to spend energy trying to have a healthy relationship with me because I can't do it right. I f**k things up. **I'm not _good_ enough** and **I'm broken and I can't be fixed** and **If people really knew me, they would go away** and **I'm stupid** and **I don't deserve _to be in a healthy relationship_** (*Boy, was I on a roll with this one. I got 5 out of 6*)
- My old cat is driving me nuts. He won't eat but is always hungry and asking for food. He climbs on everything I'm doing and knocks stuff to the ground, and I'm really tired of it. I feel like things would be better if he weren't here, then I feel like a horrible person for thinking that. **I'm not _loving_ enough** and **I don't deserve _to have a pet_**
- Grace won't return my emails or texts. I've worn out my welcome with her. She probably wishes she didn't get involved with me regarding the nonprofit. I'm more trouble than I'm worth. **My needs are less important than the needs of others** and **If people really knew me, they would go away** and **I'm not _lovable or smart_ enough** and **I'm stupid**

- Anyone who thinks I have value is stupid. **I'm stupid** and **If people really knew me, they would go away**
- I will spend the rest of my life alone. **I don't deserve _a partner_**
- I'm a worthless piece of crap. **I'm not _valuable_ enough**
- I want to break something. **I'm not _calm_ enough**
- I look old and fat. **I'm broken and I can't be fixed**
- I'm so lonely. **I don't deserve _to be in a relationship_**
- I can't do anything right. **I'm broken and I can't be fixed**
- I'm too much work. **If people really knew me, they would go away**

I've been doing this process for many years, and often I can get through the processing stages without having to write anything down. But on this particular day, I was so far gone, I needed to see my thinking in writing, clear evidence of what was tumbling around in my brain. I was batting 1000 that day. I managed to engage all of my False Core Beliefs. I was in deep.

Creating the list of thoughts wasn't hard, all I had to do was listen to what my thoughts were telling me and write them down. Identifying my False Core Beliefs was a little harder, but mostly I could find them quickly. The next stage is harder. To be honest, I've spent many hours in conversation with people I trust to help me find my way to the truth, which is the next stage in the process. One way to think of this is: *What would I say to someone I loved if they shared these things with me?* Here's what my list looked like after stage three: (underline truths are underlined)

Stage three- Tell yourself the truth

- I'm agitated, have no motivation, and feel like a fraud. Why would anyone want to read a book that I write? **I'm not _ good_ enough** <u>This is a difficult time and you can give yourself permission to not judge yourself for it. Give yourself the same compassion you would give a friend.</u>

- I have nothing to contribute that would be useful. **I'm not _smart_ enough** You have many things to do that will have value for others. It may not look the way you think it should, but that doesn't negate the value.
- I think I'm more intelligent than I am. **I'm stupid** Intelligence is relative. There are many forms of intelligence. This is your fear speaking, not truth.
- I've "snowed" a lot of people into believing that I have something valuable to contribute because I'm an actor, I can talk a good talk. **If people really knew me, they would go away.** Everyone has something to contribute. You have experience that will be valuable to some, maybe not everyone. But to those that will recognize your value, what you have to share can be life changing. And you are a good actor. It's a gift you were given, not a tool for deception
- Theater as a field is going to die because of COVID-19, and if it doesn't why would anyone even bother hiring me? **I don't deserve _a career in theater_** and **If people really knew me, they would go away** You don't know what the future will bring.
- My greatest passion as a performer, singing, is long past. My voice is shot. I can't project anymore without pain. **I'm broken and I can't be fixed** Vocal cords are a muscle, and can be toned and exercised just like any muscle. If you want to, you can get your voice back in shape.
- People don't really like me, they tolerate me. Once they know me, they don't stick around. **If people really knew me, they would go away** and **I don't deserve _good friends_** You have many friends who have been friends for decades. If you ask them for help, they would help you.
- I'm a pain in the ass, I do things wrong all the time and no one will want to spend energy trying to have a healthy relationship with me because I can't do it right. I f**k things up. **I'm not _good_ enough** and **I'm broken and I can't be fixed** and **If people really knew me, they would go away** and **I'm stu-**

pid and **I don't deserve _to be in a healthy relationship_** <u>No one is perfect. Everyone has things they don't do well.</u>

- My old cat is driving me nuts. He won't eat but is always hungry and asking for food. He climbs on everything I'm doing and knocks stuff to the ground, and I'm really tired of it. I feel like things would be better if he weren't here, then I feel like a horrible person for thinking that. **I'm not _loving_ enough** and **I don't deserve _to have a pet_** <u>Cats can be frustrating, especially when patience is worn thin because of life circumstances. He is old and just trying to be okay. He is not trying to be a pain in the ass. You're not a bad person for having negative thoughts.</u>

- Grace won't return my emails or texts. I've worn out my welcome with her. She probably wishes she didn't get involved with me regarding the nonprofit. I'm more trouble than I'm worth. **My needs are less important than the needs of others** and **If people really knew me, they would go away** and **I'm not _lovable or smart_ enough** and **I'm stupid** <u>Grace is extremely busy, and she is in pain too, and she has been through hell and back. Just because she hasn't been responding doesn't mean it's about you. In fact, it likely has nothing to do with you and she could use support herself. Even if she is upset about something, you have a good friendship that will withstand whatever obstacle is in the way.</u>

- Anyone who thinks I have value is stupid. **I'm stupid** and **If people really knew me, they would go away** <u>Wow. Okay, you don't have that much power over people, and you are not the best judge of someone else's insides, only they are.</u>

- I will spend the rest of my life alone. **I don't deserve _a partner_** <u>You are not alone</u>

- I'm a worthless piece of crap **I'm not _valuable_ enough** <u>You deserve all that is good in the world. You have value</u>

- I want to break something **I'm not _calm_ enough** <u>Go ahead, you can.</u>

- I look old and fat **I'm broken and I can't be fixed** <u>You're in your fifties and look younger than your age according to everyone else. You're heavier than you want to be but you're taking better care of yourself in other ways than you have in the past</u>
- I'm so lonely **I don't deserve _to be in a relationship_** <u>You are not alone</u>
- I can't do anything right **I'm broken and I can't be fixed** <u>You don't do everything right but you do a lot of things really well</u>
- I'm too much work **If people really knew me, they would go away** <u>You are worthy of people's love and friendship. Friendships require work to maintain them and keep them healthy. You are worth the effort.</u>

Finding the truth when negative thinking is loud can feel like mining for gold in a toilet. But the truth is there, it just needs to be revealed. At the end of this chapter, I'll provide a list of basic truths that could help you start your journey towards the truth. I can't do the job for you, because the battle is inside you, but I'll shine a light toward the way out.

The final stage of this process is a bit like a game of "find the opposite." If your negative thinking is saying one thing to you, look for the thing your negative thinking would never in a million years tell you to do, and do it. Here's what my list looked like when it was done: (**responses to engage with are bold and underlined**.)

Stage Four- Engage with a Response

- I'm agitated, have no motivation, and feel like a fraud. Why would anyone want to read a book that I write? **I'm not _ good_ enough** <u>This is a difficult time and I can give myself permission to be right where I am and not judge myself for it. Give myself the same compassion I would give a friend.</u> **Be kind to yourself. Do something nice for yourself, do something that is actively compassionate towards yourself.**

- I have nothing to contribute that would be useful. **I'm not _ smart_ enough** <u>I have many things to do that will have value for others. It may not look the way I think it should, but that doesn't negate the value.</u> **Name three things that you have done that have contributed to someone else**
- I think I'm more intelligent than I am. **I'm stupid** <u>Intelligence is relative. There are many forms of intelligence. This is fear speaking, not truth.</u> **Name three ways you undervalue yourself. If you can't find any, ask a friend.**
- I've "snowed" a lot of people into believing that I have something valuable to contribute because I'm an actor, I can talk a good talk. **If people really knew me, they would go away.** <u>Everyone has something to contribute. I have experience that will be valuable to some, maybe not everyone. But to those that will recognize my value, what I have to share can be life changing. And I am a good actor. It's a gift I was given, not a tool for deception</u> **Go do something for someone for fun and for free, that they won't recognize as something you personally have done. Value comes in the doing, not in the recognition.**
- Theater as a field is going to die because of COVID-19, and if it doesn't why would anyone even bother hiring me over someone else? **I don't deserve _a career in theater_** and **If people really knew me, they would go away** <u>I don't know what the future will bring.</u> **Let go of the need to know how things will turn out. You're not in charge of the outcome. It may well turn out better than you could possibly imagine! Meditate and breathe. Practice being in the moment.**
- My greatest passion as a performer, singing, is long past. My voice is shot. I can't project anymore without pain. **I'm broken and I can't be fixed** <u>Vocal cords are a muscle, and can be toned and exercised just like any muscle. If I want to, I can get my voice back in shape.</u> **Sing a little every day to start getting that muscle in shape again so you can sing for yourself and be happy with what comes out of your mouth.**

- People don't really like me, they tolerate me. Once they know me, they don't stick around. **If people really knew me, they would go away** and **I don't deserve _good friends_** I have many friends who have been my friends for decades. If I asked for help, they would help me. **Call someone and ask for support.**

- I'm a pain in the ass, I do things wrong all the time and no one will want to spend energy trying to have a healthy relationship with me because I can't do it right. I f**k things up. **I'm not _good_ enough** and **I'm broken and I can't be fixed** and **If people really knew me, they would go away** and **I'm stupid** and **I don't deserve _to be in a healthy relationship_** No one is perfect. Everyone has things they don't do well. **Your fear is speaking. What would you say to a friend who said this? "I love you no matter what you do, Laura!" Listen to your own words of kindness.**

Okay, you get the idea. Now, go back and look at the rest of my Stage Three examples, starting with "My old cat is driving me nuts," and come up with what you think I should do. This will help you get some practice in turning your own thinking around and finding your own responses.

When I was done doing Stage Four— giving myself an appropriate counterbalance to the negative thinking— I took the actions I assigned to myself and started doing them. As you can see, most of them were about treating myself kindly and asking for help. What did you suggest?

By the time I'd gone through all of these steps, saw what was true, and identified the story I'd been telling myself, accomplishing the list of responses was relatively easy.

If I find an action I've assigned myself difficult, I go back to the initial comment and try to break it down even further. Sometimes the story is just too powerful. When that happens it's usually because there's a lot of narrative around the feeling. I'm so invested in the story I'm telling myself that I don't want to let go. It's then that I have to describe the upset in as few words as possible. I'll use an example from my list:

- Grace won't return my emails or texts. I've worn out my welcome with her. She probably wishes she didn't get involved with me regarding the nonprofit. I'm more trouble than I'm worth.

There's a lot of story around this upset. I read it over and over and tried to find the shortest way to say it. I came down to this:

- I'm afraid that Grace doesn't want to be my friend.

So clear. The rest of the story falls away and I can see exactly which False Core Belief is snared: **If people really knew me, they would go away.** The truth is <u>she loves me</u>. The response I chose was to call her. I called and told her that I love her and said if there was anything I could do to support her, she just needed to ask.

Here's something you're not going to want to hear—your False Core Beliefs aren't going anywhere. They're part of you. But they'll have less power over you if you can identify the thinking. They'll be more like ink on a page that has faded in the sunlight. You can still read it, but it's less vibrant. Just do your best to keep revealing them for what they are: false.

You may find it difficult to turn a thought around or find an appropriate response. Flipping your thoughts and finding an authentic response isn't going to come from a list I give you. It'll come from your gut, but here are some more examples to get your thoughts around it flowing:

Recognize the Thought:	Identify the False Core Belief:
1-I really blew it. I can never make this right.	I'm an idiot.
2-I'll never find a partner.	I don't deserve to be loved.
3-I'm pissed about the dent in my car, and the person didn't leave a note. I hate the world.	Nothing ever goes right, *and* I don't matter.
4-I'm so scared about the crime in my neighborhood, but I can't afford to move.	I'm not safe, *and* my needs don't matter.
5-My mother never says she's proud of me. I try so hard but it's like I'm invisible.	I'm unlovable, *and* I'm worthless, *and* everyone I love goes away.
6-I never do anything right.	I'm broken.

Tell Yourself the Truth:	Engage with a Response:
1-Everyone makes mistakes. You aren't perfect, you're human.	Forgive yourself for not being perfect. Is there anything that needs fixing? If so, fix it.
2-The future is unknown. There is a right person for everyone. You deserve to find yours.	Call a friend and plan something fun with them where you might meet new people.
3-Accidents happen. People can be very inconsiderate, but it doesn't mean anything about you. Go ahead, be mad. It sucks.	Write a letter to that person telling them exactly how you feel. Then destroy the letter in a way that would feel satisfying.
4-Everyone deserves to be safe, even you. Determine if you're feeling unsafe in the moment or because of something that happened in the past. If you're in danger right now, you get to be safe. Take care of yourself.	Is there something you can do to make yourself feel safer, like add more locks to your door? Call the Housing Authority and see if there are other options for moving that you might not have thought about.
5-Don't judge yourself based on someone else's opinions or reactions. It likely has nothing to do with you at all but stems from their own False Core Beliefs. You deserve to be seen and congratulated for your accomplishments.	Call a trusted friend and tell them how you are feeling. Make of list of what you're proud of and share it with them. Write "Congratulation, you're amazing!" on a piece of paper and put it up where you'll see it.
6-That is a generalization and simply not the truth. You may make mistakes, everyone does. That's normal.	Look at the last 24 hours. Make a list of everything you did right. Congratulate yourself for a job well done.

~ Staying in the Moment ~

I'm an overachiever in the worst ways. And when I don't do things "right" I have terribly destructive negative self-talk, even about inconsequential things. I recently had an epiphany about something that has caused a dramatic shift in understanding how my trauma has manifested in my body and the way I see myself.

During a group session with other survivors, our facilitator was leading us in a grounding exercise where she asked us to breathe in deeply and hold our breath for as long or as little as we wanted. Then she said, "Even a breath can be triggering, so do what feels right." My first thought was, "How could a breath be triggering, it's a breath, it's life!" Then it dawned on me that I hold my breath when I'm scared. It's something I've always done.

Because I have difficulty falling asleep, I often listen to guided Yoga Nidra meditations before bed. In some of the exercises the guide instructs the listener to take a deep breath and hold it for several seconds, and every time I hear it, I have resistance that can vary from mild annoyance to outright panic.

Being a good follower of instructions, I used to do the breathing technique as suggested regardless of how it caused my anxiety to skyrocket. In the past few years though, I started allowing myself to skip holding my breath as part of any guided meditation and just continue deep breathing that isn't interrupted. I had private shame that this breath-holding technique, which was clearly a great way for some people to release tension, was a source of anxiety for me. I'd have shaming conversations in my head around it, telling myself I was weak or strange for not being able to do something as simple as a breath exercise properly.

I didn't understand why my body was reacting like that until the facilitator talked about breath being triggering for some people. Now I get it—I realized that every time I was raped, I'd held my breath. In two instances, my abuser actually put their hand over my mouth. Of course, breath could be a trigger!

A flood of self-compassion washed over me. I was relieved that I was able to take care of myself in this simple way. I saw that giving myself permission to no longer silently torture myself by following instructions, that no one would ever even know I wasn't following anyway, was a form of self-care, and evidence of how I'm beginning to instinctively honor my body in a way I never used to.

Now I get to decide what to do with this information. The old me could have taken this little tidbit as more evidence of how messed up I am. "Oh great, now I get to be triggered by my own breath, which I do all day long, every day. I'll never escape this!"

Well, well, well, doesn't that ring a bell—*I'm broken and I can't be fixed.* I do a quick inventory for RITE Thinking:

Stage One- *Recognize the thought*
Even breath is a trigger. I'll never escape this!

Stage Two- *Identify the False Core Belief*
I'm broken and I can't be fixed.

Stage Three- *Tell yourself the truth*
Breath is a gift. This epiphany is a gift. I get to recognize something about myself, see it for what it is, and make a conscious choice about what to do with this information. I deserve to take care of myself.

Stage Four- *Engage with a response*
I choose to allow this new awareness to establish a new neural pathway that leads to gratitude for my body and not shame.

I decided that every time I recognize this breath issue, I'm going to thank my body for taking care of me and have gratitude for my ability to choose to breathe out when someone tells me to hold my breath. I'll celebrate the rebellion of doing it my own way! A simple decision that has had a deeply profound impact.

We have a choice about where to focus our energy when we gain new awareness. We can lean away from old patterns and lean into healing. We can use what we gather as evidence for old thinking, a positive reinforcement of a negative belief, or we can use it to establish a new place for our thinking to go. That's what Neuroplasticity is all about.[28]

When you walk in wet grass you can look back and see where you walked because your feet leave an imprint. After the grass dries, and the wind blows, you may not see the path anymore. It hasn't been well enough established to withstand the elements that make that grass go back to the way it was. But if you keep walking on that same line every day for a month, a clear path will form because of the repeated motion of stomping down the grass. It's the same thing with our thoughts. They'll strengthen whatever path they're on.

The RITE Thinking Process is an opportunity to strengthen our use of the 3 A's in our daily lives. R (recognize the thought) and I (identify the False Core Belief) = awareness, T (tell yourself the truth) = acceptance, and E (engage with a response) = action. Using this tool regularly will help you stay in the moment when things come up.

~ Widening the Lens~

Bravo to you for coming this far. This isn't easy. Well done!

The beauty of the three A's lives in their simplicity. They're straightforward, no-nonsense. They're easy to understand but can be extremely difficult to implement. After reading through Part One, investigating your False Core Beliefs, and learning about the RITE Thinking Process, it's my sincere wish that you've been able to gather some new awareness around your thoughts and how you're participating in your relationships. Sticking with thinking that no longer serves us can keep us locked in unhealthy behavior patterns. I hope you see the possibilities, of how changing the way we engage with our thoughts can allow us to alter behaviors.

---

[28] Neuroplasticity: noun; the ability of the brain to form and reorganize synaptic connections, especially in response to learning, or experience, or following injury. Oxford Languages

In the next part of this book, we'll look beyond the edges of our thinking and towards a wider perspective. I invite you to carry what you've learned about your personal False Core Beliefs with you now as I widen the lens, to see how they can show up in relation to social constructs and social contracts.

Part Two

Transforming Culture

Chapter Seven

Shedding Willful Ignorance

We can evolve as individuals, to alter our thinking for the better, no matter how old we are. Changing behaviors is not only possible but also attainable if we truly desire a different outcome and commit ourselves to health and wellness.

I believe this is true for transforming culture as well. Using the 3 A's and the insights gained in Part One of this book can point us in the direction of how we're participating in our lives in the larger context of cultural norms.

This might feel a little terrifying and sound exhausting. I get it—I feel it too. Every time I hear another story about a predatory athletic coach getting away with assaulting athletes, or children dying because some mentally unstable person brought a gun into an elementary school, I think, "What's the point? Nothing is ever going to change. We just keep moving backward."

But here's some truth: it won't be one big thing that changes the road we're on, no single law that will fix the problem. It's billions of actions, all of us, making choices in big and small ways. When you need to rest from fighting the good fight, rest by all means, take a break. And when you're ready, get back at it. The world needs you to be in action.

We have a choice about where we want to focus our energy, and where we want to spend our hard-earned money. These things matter. We do have the power to create change but it's going to take time and commitment.

Rape Culture is at the heart of the issues I've battled in my own life—I'm going to focus primarily on this destructive social contract in this part of this book.

rape cul·ture[29]
noun
A society or environment whose prevailing social attitudes have the effect of normalizing or trivializing sexual assault and abuse.

Our society is built on a collection of social contracts and social constructs. Sometimes the line between the two is very blurry. Simply put, here is how I distinguish between them.

Social Contracts are agreements we consent to, consciously or unconsciously:

- Taking turns
- Following laws
- Believing women and minorities are inferior
- Assuming being "white" makes one superior
- Rape Culture

Social contracts aren't inherently bad— waiting to get on a bus or elevator until others have gotten off is a social contract that prevents chaos. But *not* calling someone out when they tell a rape joke or say the "n-word" is a social contract we can do without. All too often we don't address issues like this because we're afraid to upset the status quo.[30]

Social Constructs are concepts and categories established by collective agreement, consciously or unconsciously:

- Paper money
- The meaning of words
- Standards of beauty
- Ownership of property
- Race

---

[29] Oxford Languages
[30] Status Quo- noun: the existing state of affairs, especially regarding social or political issues. Oxford Languages

Social constructs aren't based on truth, they're based on agreements, good or bad. Paper money has power because we all agree that it does— really, it's just paper. Standards of beauty have power, not because being "beautiful" makes someone powerful, but because we *give* those considered beautiful power— she is prettier, so she is better.

Harmful social constructs are embedded in our society, often established by people in positions of power, and have existed for as long as we can remember. Some social contracts allow harmful social constructs to prevail, upholding destructive behaviors of people and institutions, and making them feel justified in their continued dominance over those considered weaker or "less than."

Altering social contracts feels downright impossible, especially when we're talking about these issues because they have a strong foundation that will be difficult to dismantle. There have been movements in the past that have tried to change these narratives and failed.

The focus of this chapter is Rape Culture, but what is said here can apply to multiple destructive forces that run parallel to it, such as gender inequality and racism.

Before we get too much deeper into this conversation, there are some additional social precepts that should be put forward. Cisgender[31] women are not the only ones who get raped— sexual violence knows no boundaries. Boys and girls are both vulnerable to sexual exploitation. Males and females of any age are capable of being perpetrators. The vast majority of sexual predators are men, but both men and women contribute to upholding Rape Culture. Though this section of the book more frequently discusses the effects of Rape Culture on women, it should not be considered comprehensive or exclusionary of all who are be impacted— male, female, non-binary, transgendered, young, old, able bodied, disabled, etc.

We all participate in Rape Culture, but it's a harsh reality that men have been the primary contributors to it. This is not true in

---

[31] Cisgender- denoting or relating to a person whose gender identity corresponds with the sex registered for them at birth; not transgender.

every society. The historical ideals of some of the Native American communities are starkly different in this respect from Western ideology. In fact, before North America was colonized by Europeans, many Indigenous women held power within their tribes and could participate in their society equal to men. And genderfluidity was embraced, even considered sacred by some, such as Two-Spirit individuals.[32] Since colonization, that script has flipped and Indigenous women are one of the most vulnerable groups when it comes to sexual violence.

Sadly, this section of the book shines an unflattering light on how men, primarily white men, have behaved regarding power and dominance for centuries. (Thankfully, not all men behave poorly, and without the allyship of men, women's rights wouldn't have evolved as they have.) Many destructive behaviors exhibited by men stem from unspoken social contracts that have been handed down over generations. We tend to simply follow suit and not question these kinds of legacies. With fresh light shed on what this patriarchal legacy has manifested, people may realize they have a choice about how they move forward regarding Rape Culture.

There's content in this section of the book that may push you, hook you, make you uncomfortable. Investigating your thinking process in the first part of this book may have challenged you, but this section asks you now to look at how you participate in your own life in a way you may never have. And show you some things that are hard to look at. You'll probably have some strong feelings—it's to be expected. Take care of yourself as you go, but don't let any fear of seeing what's true stop you.

---

[32] Identifying as Two-Spirit is a term and concept rooted in Indigenous cultures in North America, primarily among Native American, First Nations, and Indigenous peoples. Two-Spirit is a term used to describe a person who embodies both masculine and feminine qualities, often encompassing a spiritual and gender identity outside the binary understanding of male and female.

~ Awareness: What exactly is Rape Culture? ~

Rape Culture is a set of attitudes and behaviors that perpetuate and normalize rape as an acceptable or even inevitable part of life. It's one of the most harmful and destructive social contracts that exists in our society.

We've been fed a way of thinking and participating in the world around us that reinforces negative social norms and mores. For survivors of sexual violence, this keeps us locked into the effects of our trauma and we don't recognize it— we may feel a twinge of something being wrong, but go no further in our investigation of why we felt it. This is the power of culture.

In the United States, women still don't have full agency over their bodies, in fact, our rights are under attack. Because the Equal Rights Amendment (ERA) was never ratified in 1982 as it could have been, the rights of women in the United States aren't a given. Fascinatingly, the ERA movement wasn't squashed by men as one might think; that charge was led by Phyllis Schlafly, an outspoken conservative woman, demonstrating how social contracts that hold the rights of women back are supported from multiple angles, and have been for a very long time.

How are we supposed to get people to stop supporting social contracts like Rape Culture when they are so deeply embedded in everyday life? Answer: This is a long game. In order to effectively shift the culture around us in a permanent way, we need to be willing to look at how we participate in it. Most people aren't aware of how they contribute to the problem, but we all do. If we can break free of this normalized way of being and put our efforts towards normalizing a Culture of Consent, it would change many of our problems at the root.

Rape Culture is a relatively new term in our common lexicon, but it was coined during the feminist movement of the 1970s. If we want to irradicate it, we must first understand that it's a system of silencing entrenched in our society. The pilings go deep into the bedrock of our psyches. When we step away from that structure and defy its legitimacy it begins to falter. As is the case with systems of oppression, it's not going away without a fight, and it sings its sweet song of denial, calling us back to the familiar comfort of our discomfort because it needs us to stay where we are so *it* won't fall down.

A lack of awareness and understanding leads to a lack of compassion. And if you don't have foundational information about these things, how can you make autonomous and educated choices? How can you fight an enemy you know nothing about? We must understand the dynamics around sexual violence if we want to create change. The following description from Marshall U* provides an excellent definition:

> Rape Culture is an environment in which rape is prevalent and in which sexual violence against women is normalized and excused in the media and popular culture. Rape Culture is perpetuated through the use of misogynistic language, the objectification of women's bodies, and the glamorization of sexual violence, thereby creating a society that disregards women's rights and safety.
>
> Rape Culture affects every woman. The rape of one woman is a degradation, terror, and limitation to all women. Most women and girls limit their behavior because of the existence of rape. Most women and girls live in fear of rape. Men, in general, do not. That's how rape functions as a powerful means by which the whole female population is held in a subordinate position to the whole male population, even though most men don't rape and many women are never victims of rape. This cycle of fear is the legacy of Rape Culture.
>
> Examples of Rape Culture:
>
> - Blaming the victim (She asked for it)
> - Trivializing sexual assault (Boys will be boys)
> - Sexually explicit jokes
> - Tolerance of sexual harassment
> - Inflating false rape report statistics

- Publicly scrutinizing a victim's dress, mental state, motives, and history
- Gratuitous gendered violence in movies and television
- Defining "manhood" as dominant and sexually aggressive.
- Defining "womanhood" as submissive and sexually passive
- Pressure on men to "score"
- Pressure on women to not appear "cold"
- Assuming only promiscuous women get raped
- Assuming that men don't get raped or that only "weak" men get raped
- Refusing to take rape accusations seriously
- Teaching women to avoid getting raped instead of teaching men not to rape

As a woman, I recognize the historical harm that's been inflicted on women and those who identify as female or feminine. I feel it in my body, like an electrical current. It's not the specific energy I carry as a sexual assault survivor, but it's born of the same generator because sexual violence isn't just about sex, it's about power—finding, claiming, or utilizing power, whether physical or psychological. It's important that we understand the dynamics around sexual violence if we want to create change.

Cultural shift doesn't just happen. The evolution of society grows from the small ways we allow ourselves to be transformed, which then colors the way we are with each other. Ignorance allows us to hide from the realities of the prevalence of sexual harm in the world. Gaining awareness and understanding of Rape Culture and seeing how we participate in it is the key to pushing the cultural shift from complicity to accountability.

Challenges to changing Rape Culture include:

- Lack of understanding - Not enough information and dismissive attitudes.
- Willful ignorance - It's easier to look away than to see what's true.

- Power structures - Upholding male dominance and fearing the power of women.
- Shock and disregard - Disbelief or discrediting victims when the truth is spoken.
- Language - Media misrepresentation, rape jokes, victim blaming.

Transforming Rape Culture requires:

- **Awareness** - Stop ignoring the truth about what's happening around you. See how you participate in Rape Culture—because we all do.
- **Acceptance** - Sexual violence is real, and it's not pretty. Allow yourself to really look at what's in the shadows. Not looking doesn't make it go away, it helps to keep it hidden, which helps support the system that holds Rape Culture in place. Accept the reality of what we're up against.
- **Action** - Be willing to be uncomfortable. Step outside of your comfort zone. Use your personal autonomy and your voice to affect change and encourage others to do so too. Insist on accountability.

~ #MeToo ~

The #MeToo movement, founded by Tarana Burke[33] in 2006, was catapulted to national awareness in 2017 by the women in Hollywood who called out producer Harvey Weinstein as a sexual predator. #MeToo set something in motion that has never before occurred—undeniable public awareness of the way women are widely treated and have been treated since the dawn of time.

---

[33] Tarana coined the term #MeToo to bring awareness in the black community to violence against black and brown women. The term went viral in 2017 bringing attention to sexual violence against all women. I lift up her name, her story, and acknowledge the double-jeopardy that exists for women of color. To learn more about the origins of the movement visit https://metoomvmt.org/get-to-know-us/history-inception/

#MeToo cracked open something in society that was long overdue and a tidal wave of truth-telling swept through our society. The movement called attention to the despicable and disgusting actions of Weinstein and his ilk, the people who enabled them, and the culture that normalizes this kind of oppressive, abusive, and demeaning behavior.

Because of #MeToo, women in general are less willing now to accept unacceptable behavior. Many men are reflecting on their own participation in cultivating this cultural blemish, and are discovering they've played a part in it by riding on the entitlement that goes with their gender. They're starting to see the ways they've trampled the emotional and physical barriers women have been trying to uphold for themselves, and women are seeing the ways they themselves have continually moved the lines of personal safe space to conform or not make waves. It's a new era. But it's not enough.

#MeToo is one of the most important societal reckonings that has happened in our generation; It permitted half the population of our planet to take a collective breath and exhale truth in the form of a shared experience. Not all women chose to take advantage of that wave of truth-telling, but by defining sexual violence to include not only rape and attempted rape but also unwanted or non-consensual sexual contact, sexual harassment, and sexual exploitation, all women can recognize its presence in their lives.

#MeToo isn't just about cisgender girls and women. Gender nonconforming[34] and transgender[35] individuals have their own place in this tragic legacy. Members of these communities are vulnerable, misunderstood, and despised by a huge portion of our society, and are frequent targets for bigotry and violence. According to the Office

---

[34] Gender nonconforming: exhibiting behavioral, cultural, or psychological traits that do not correspond with the traits typically associated with one's sex: having a gender expression that does not conform to gender norms. Merriam-Webster. com

[35] Transgender : of, relating to, or being a person whose gender identity is opposite the sex the person had or was identified as having at birth. Merriam-Webster. com

for Victims of Crime report, sixty-six percent of transgender individuals have experienced sexual violence.[36]

We must also take a moment to address the unique aspects of sexual violence against men, and the hurdles men face when trying to find healing—they face a stigma that women don't. Being a "man" comes along with a social contract that is placed on boys long before they understand what any of it means. What they do understand is that they can't be seen as weak, lest they be considered "unmanly."

I did my best while raising my two boys to teach them that their emotions matter. But that commitment didn't erase the social contract, so even though they were getting messages at home that allowed them to step away from destructive social norms, they still had friends, advertising, media messaging, films, and television perpetuating that old narrative. It's impossible to escape.

This social programming makes it very hard for men to reach for help when it comes to emotional, psychological, or physical abuse. When you believe you must be strong at all costs, it goes against the grain to disclose abuse, especially sexual abuse. Males fear asking for help because they don't want to be seen as weak. Instead, our message to them should be: you matter as much as anyone else. Please reach out for help so you can receive the gift of healing. You deserve it.

One last thing on #MeToo: the benefits of this movement have not reached into every corner of society; It hasn't been a magic wand that changed everything for the better. There are still people who suffer from sexual violence, there is still ignorance and unwillingness to shift behavior. But #MeToo has provided an awakening, a pivotal moment in our culture that will shape the work ahead.

~ The Part We All Play ~

Some women of my mother's generation roll their eyes at younger generations who speak out about sexual harassment because they

---

[36] https://ovc.ojp.gov/sites/g/files/xyckuh226/files/pubs/forge/sexual_numbers.html NOTE: The Trump Administration has since removed this Department of Justice reference page referring to violent crimes against transgendered people.

tolerated so much of it throughout their lives. No one encouraged them to make a stink about it. They were told to deal with it because "you won't get far if you make a fuss." Harassment is everywhere, so why try?

Sometimes bystanders of harm stand slack-jawed at the boldness of people who perpetrate harm, from offenses such as rape jokes all the way to public demonstrations of physical abuse. Sometimes they stay silent because they're afraid to say something, but also because they're in shock and don't snap out of it.

Here's an ugly truth. A male friend told me he'd been sexually assaulted by a respected member of our community. I believed him, of course. He had no reason to lie to me. Despite that, my first thought was, "I wonder if it was just touching, or was he raped?" Followed by, "We should find out if there were others so it'll add legitimacy to his claim, otherwise it's not as valid."

It pains me that these thoughts would ever enter my mind. This is how deeply Rape Culture can be embedded in those who are victim-survivors themselves. We have all been programmed to downgrade sex crimes. One might hear about a gang rape and immediately wonder, "How many guys did it. Five? Ten?" As if the number matters. Isn't one enough? One is one too many.

The prevailing narrative that men are better than, smarter than, and stronger than women was handed to us all centuries ago, and it controls us in obvious and covert ways. In her book *Women and Power*, Mary Beard points to the first literary example of the squashing of women in power, which appears in Homer's *The Odyssey* written in the 8th century BCE. When Queen Penelope of Ithaca tries to speak to a group of men that her son, the teenage Telemachus, is speaking to, he basically tells his mother to shut up and go to her room, which she does. And she is the ruler of the country! We have thousands of years of silencing women at our backs.

In Elizabeth Lesser's *Cassandra Speaks*—a highly recommended book that examines and champions the female collective voice—the author refers to a stomach-turning passage from the Book of Ecclesiasticus. It reads:

A gift from the Lord is a silent wife,
And nothing is so precious as her self-discipline.
Charm upon charm is a wife with a sense of shame,
And nothing is more valuable than her bound-up mouth.

Women are up against a centuries-old incessant narrative that holds men in positions of power, one that is bold and obvious, but also camouflaged with altruism. We still have to deal with puffed-up men belittling women in public ways, supported by respected entities.

The Wall Street Journal printed an Op-Ed by an older white man who publicly called on First Lady, Dr. Jill Biden, to stop using "doctor" in her name because she isn't a medical doctor. He even had the audacity to call this highly educated, mature woman "kiddo" in his essay. When called out by the public outrage, the editor, another older white man, stood by his decision to run the essay. As one of this man's critics put it, that piece never would have been printed if it had asked a man to remove a title that gave evidence of his accomplishment. But here we are.

Those who are deeply invested in Rape Culture aren't giving up without a fight. Power-hungry men commonly use their inherited entitlement by dominating those considered weaker. They do it in every space, from boardrooms to bedrooms. Marginalized members of society, such as women, children, LGBTQ, BIPOC, the unhoused, the elderly, and the differently abled are the easy targets for dominance. This practice provides an easy path to a sense of superiority for someone wanting to feel the surge of hormones that comes with exerting power over another. And there have been little to no barriers for these predators as far as society and the judicial system are concerned. Sexual crimes go unpunished 99% of the time, while thousands of unprocessed rape kits sit in storage rooms across this country, allowing rapists to continue their quest for power through dominance.

Sexual predators rely on the ignorance of society and the upholding of Rape Culture to get away with their crimes. Sometimes there are respected traditions that keep us from seeing what's true.

A few years back, my hometown of Minneapolis hosted the Super Bowl. At the time, I worked at the Guthrie Theater a few blocks from the stadium. My biggest concern was road congestion and parking in the area. Theater management told us not to come in, no shows were scheduled in the days around the game. Downtown was going to be packed.

Several months prior to the "big game," I was getting some therapeutic body work done by a dear friend who is a massage therapist. During the session, we chatted about her new location as well as the fact that she recently had to go through the renewal of her license, which she found frustrating because it was sooner than it normally would have been scheduled. I asked why that was and she explained they were cracking down on massage therapists to make sure they were legitimate because Minneapolis was hosting the Super Bowl. Not putting two and two together, I asked, "What does massage therapy have to do with the Super Bowl?" Her response was, "Sex trafficking." I was stunned. How did I not know this?

She went on to explain that every single city that hosts the Super Bowl goes through this. Because of the number of men that come to town to attend the game, it's a huge money maker for sex trafficking rings who often set up shop under the guise of massage parlors. My concern about parking was nothing compared to the realities of sex trafficking. The fact that this is common knowledge for some people and off the radar for others is horrific to me. I'll never look at the Super Bowl the same way again.

Human sex trafficking happens everywhere, in every state, province, every country in the world. This isn't a QAnon conspiracy, it doesn't affect only one political party, it's not just men involved in the abuse, women do it too. Trafficking and the production of child sexual abuse images is a multi-billion-dollar industry, and it's not going away anytime soon. This is a harsh reality.

These kinds of networks operate very covertly and are well hidden, so it's not surprising that most people don't know about them. If they were more obvious, they wouldn't be successful. Their success is dependent on secrecy and silence.

News media doesn't like to amplify facts like this. People don't want to hear about it on the evening news because when we're tucking our kids in at night, we don't want to be thinking about the fact that children are taken off the streets in this country and forced into sex trafficking. The truth is ugly. Ignoring it is easier than being present to uncomfortable realities that hit a little too close to home, like the fact that some immigrant children who were separated from their parents at the Mexican border ended up being trafficked for sex. Too many of us employ our privilege of being able to look away because it's too much to take. This kind of complicity allows Rape Culture to endure.

People are witness to public displays of physical harm and offensive rape jokes and do nothing, say nothing. Sometimes they're in shock— *Did I really hear what I just heard?* — or they're too afraid to speak up. They freeze in the moment they should spring into action. They forget and move on. Or they don't see the relevance of why it should be different because it doesn't affect them directly.

Trump being elected as president in 2016, after being called out as a sexual predator, sends a clear message that millions of people don't hold the safety of women as a priority. We've been trained to downgrade sexual violence as something to be tolerated, even expected. It's part of the package so why make a big deal out of it?

However, many enlightened individuals found this explanation unacceptable, which may explain why the most powerful social reckoning of our generation, the #MeToo movement, was able to open a floodgate a year later. Those who hold the truth that women's safety is a human right, not a luxury, were pushed to speak like never before. While Trump's rhetoric may have emboldened a section of our society to declare their superiority over women, it also unleashed a collective voice that will not be silenced. We're finding strength in numbers.

~ Messaging ~

We have been inundated with the messaging of Rape Culture from the day we were born. The messaging has been powerful and incessant.

In the home, girls are told if a boy hits them or pulls their hair that means he likes them. Effect: girls grow into women who believe they must accept harmful behavior. Boys are told they must be strong all the time. "Big boys don't cry." Effect: Boys grow into men who believe emotions are something to avoid.

News, magazines, the internet, film, misogynistic video gaming, and TV are the prime culprits for messaging that strengthens Rape Culture because they continually send messages that devalue women and the female experience. Today there are encouraging examples of alternative messaging—TV shows and films that have strong female characters for instance—but they're sandwiched between scads of other shows and advertising that sell a different story. You can see it on the evening news—you don't even need to have the sound on. What do you see when you turn on your local news? Typically, it's an older white man sitting next to a beautiful younger woman, usually blonde.[37] One rarely sees a female news anchors with grey hair[38], and they are the outliers.

When women age, we lose our appeal—at least that's what the media would have us believe—perpetuating a story that devalues women as they mature. Women are still being told they need to lose weight for roles in theater, film, and TV, and that they must stay young-looking and beautiful. Then these same women are chastised for using anti-aging processes like Botox. One minute you hear, "Why doesn't she just let herself age gracefully?" Then the next "Well, she sure isn't aging well." It's a lose/lose scenario.

Strong men are considered good leaders. Strong women are considered bitchy and ambitious. If a man shows his strength, he's applauded for having grit. If a woman shows her strength, she's chastised for trying to be something she's not or told she's not likable.

---

[37] Sometimes a station will tick one of their diversity boxes and hire people of color for those chairs.

[38] Highly respected Canadian news anchor Lisa LaFlamme decided to let her hair go grey during the pandemic. She was fired with no clear reason from her job at CTV in June 2022 after a successful thirty-five-year career. The company's public reason for letting her go was stated as "business reasons."

All these narratives support Rape Culture. They strengthen the idea that men are more valuable than women. They uphold beliefs and actions that keep women in a place of subjugation to men. Women are kept from feeling ownership over their intrinsic strengths, and from claiming their rightful place in positions of power typically held by men.

Though some of the messaging is changing for the better, young women still pay attention to how older women are treated—it affects them. Some in the younger generation, both male and female, are calling out the ridiculous standards, and it gives one hope that we're headed in the right direction.

I believe some in the media are trying to do better by victim-survivors, and even in that, they don't always get it right. There was a magazine article written in 2018, about the impending trial and the man who raped me and several other women when we were children. Trying to give a balanced perspective, my perpetrator was interviewed and given a public platform, in which he denied his guilt, saying his victims pursued him, calling us "libidos in training."[39] This man had sold all his assets and fled the country to avoid being held responsible for his actions in civil court. And yet the editors had made his full interview accessible to readers online, beyond what was used in the article, because this serial rapist had made it a condition of being interviewed. I didn't even know about this condition until I saw a link to his full interview when the article was published online. His victims weren't given the same courtesy of access to their personal narratives. I had to call the editor myself to get them to give access to the public to read my full responses to the interview. Not only is this unbalanced, it's in no way trauma-informed.

Why does a sexual assault survivor have to fight to be heard when a criminal can get his rantings published by simply asking? Why did the editor not immediately think they should provide balance for the victims? Why did the female author of the article, knowing all along

---

[39] Minneapolis St. Paul Magazine article entitled *The Exit Strategy* - May 2018 edition

that this predator's rant would be published in full, not insist that the editor give the women she interviewed for the article the same courtesy? Answer: Rape Culture.

~ The Backlog ~

Back around 2015, news about a backlog of unprocessed Sexual Assault Kits (SAKs) in the United States began making headlines. The reality of just how many SAKs were sitting in storage around the country began unfolding. Well over 100,000 untested kits have been found in hidden spaces collecting dust. And many more never even made it to a storage facility because they were discarded. Each of these kits represents a human being. I have some personal experience with the Sexual Assault Kit Initiative (SAKI) that may shed some light on the subject.

In 2022, I worked for the Sexual Violence Center in Minneapolis as a Rape Crisis Advocate. In addition to my duties as a community advocate, I served as part of the Multi-Disciplinary Team (MDT) tasked with investigating each of the SAKs in the backlog for the city of Minneapolis. The SAKI team included attorneys and legal advocates from the Hennepin County Attorney's Office (HCAO), current and former officers from the Minneapolis Police Department (MPD) as investigators, and the Bureau of Criminal Apprehension (BCA) lab. I was the only member of a community-based organization on the team.

The MPD was under intense scrutiny, being the entity that had employed Officer Derek Chauvin, the man who murdered George Floyd in May of 2020. I'd gone to middle school with the Chief of Police, Medaria Arradondo, and I have deep respect for him as a person and consider him a good friend. I know him to be a man of great integrity and he was an excellent police officer. But I also know a police department is bigger than one man. The Police Officer's Union is very strong and has historically protected problematic officers. I didn't know what I would find or how I would be received by the SAKI team.

I was apprehensive at first, not knowing what their understanding of trauma-informed care was, or if my advocacy for victim-survivors would be respected. As I got to know this group of mostly women, I found them to be deeply committed, thoughtful, caring, and wanting to do the right thing for victim-survivors. I was relieved. (By the end of my time with the SAKI team I'd grown a deep respect for each of them, and they me.)

Starting from the baseline that everyone has the right to know what happened to their evidence, we dug into all the information available to us. We wanted to know not only what had happened at the time of the incident, but also where victim-survivors were now. We considered what would be the best way for them to receive this information. Sometimes they were now living in another state and we needed to find them.

The majority of the cases concerned people who are traditionally underserved and in vulnerable communities: unhoused, drug addicts, alcoholics, mentally unstable, sex workers, teenagers, and women of color. Some of the victim-survivors were sexually promiscuous, for whom assumptions were regularly made about their behavior. Some had been incarcerated before and their credibility was questioned.

Investigating each SAK was arduous. Equal consideration was given to each case, with ample time allotted to decide when and if we would notify a victim-survivor that their SAK was in the backlog. We considered all knowable aspects of the current situation of victim-survivors. A decision to not notify was made in cases where the team believed the information would be more harmful than helpful. For instance, if we knew a victim- survivor was in a mental health institution, this new information might be more damaging than helpful to their already fragile mental state. Those cases would be set aside and kept for possible future notification.

Even if the victim was deceased, it was investigated by the team. Every case was a piece of a gigantic puzzle and deserved to be examined. Sometimes a case would have connecting threads to another case, so it all mattered. We found survivors with multiple perpetrators, and perpetrators with multiple victims.

Notifying and advocating for SAKI survivors is an intensely difficult job. Often, the survivors were completely unaware their kit was never processed. Having provided evidence and given a statement regarding their assault, they naturally assumed some action had been taken.

For some, hearing that their SAK was in the backlog and was now being looked at was a relief. They were happy to know something was being done, and it brought them a sense of closure after so much time not knowing what happened to their investigation. Others found the notification devastating—a re-traumatization. To be assaulted and then discarded by the entity that was supposed to be fighting for them added insult to injury. It seemed the farther back in time the rape happened, the deeper the cut when they found out their kit was in the backlog. The oldest case I read was from 1998.

While reading through case files, certain reasons emerged as to why some of these kits didn't make it to a lab. One was the lack of response or cooperation from the victim-survivor during the investigation. If a victim-survivor stopped communicating with the investigating officer, the case could be deemed "closed" and the SAK could be put into storage.

Criminal investigations are very painful. It takes a lot out of a victim-survivor to allow such transparency around something so devastating as a rape. PTSD can make it impossible. If a victim-survivor doesn't feel seen or respected by a first responder or investigating officer, it's easy for them to retreat into the shadows and stop communicating with police.

Sometimes written statements made by responding officers or investigators displayed an obvious negative bias, and I wasn't surprised that certain SAKs ended up in the backlog—the lack of respect for the victim-survivor was blatant. I grew disgusted with the dismissive language and behaviors I saw in some of those old reports. It was clear the officer either didn't believe the victim-survivor, or thought the victim was somehow responsible for what happened to them, or didn't see the case as solvable. They didn't treat the victim-survivors with respect, or understand how trauma works. Often you would see the same officer's name on multiple reports for SAKI survivors whose kits landed in the backlog.

Thankfully we know more about trauma now, and officers are receiving at least some trauma-informed training—one of the most compassionate responses to a rape victim-survivor I've ever witnessed came from an officer receiving a report. It was extraordinary to see how validating it is for a victim-survivor to be seen compassionately by someone in a position of authority. But as an advocate, I still saw officers who were dismissive of the men and women I accompanied as they gave their police reports. A caring space matters so much when you're at your most vulnerable. When an officer appreciates the courage it takes to disclose, and shows a victim-survivor that they care, that is a real gift.

Further complicating the issue, some SAKs are considered restricted and are not sent to a lab for processing. The choice to restrict a SAK is made by the victim-survivor— the evidence is collected at the hospital, but the victim-survivor states they do not want the kit processed at that time. A victim-survivor may be in shock and not know whether or not they want to press charges, so they can request that the kit be kept but not processed until they can decide later what they want to do with that evidence. These restricted SAKs were put in storage, and therefore ended up in the backlog if the victim-survivor never pressed charges.

The backlog of SAKs is an effect of Rape Culture. It's a symptom of a larger problem. It speaks to the widespread lack of trauma-informed care in policing, and bears witness to a judicial system that is slanted in favor of sexual predators.

In an attempt to prevent a future backlog of SAKs, the Minnesota State Legislature passed a law in 2022 requiring all unrestricted SAKs to be picked up by law enforcement within ten days of notification by the hospital where a kit is collected. The police agency then has sixty days to submit the kit to the lab for testing.

During my time with SAKI, Minneapolis was experiencing high rates of violent crimes, car-jackings in particular. The BCA lab put a hold on processing SAKs in order to prioritize other crimes, which drew a lot of negative media attention[40]. Why would the BCA do that? The answer would seem to be because Rape Culture doesn't prioritize women's health and safety. Victims of sexual violence, primarily women, are left hanging, and the perpetrators, mostly men, aren't held accountable for their actions. It's a tale as old as time.

Though I know amazing police officers, lawyers, and advocates who are trauma-informed and doing incredible work for victim-survivors of sexual violence, sadly, not everyone in the system gets it.

~ Awareness Reality Check ~

Here's a shocking reality to help put this in perspective: If 1 in 5 children are sexually assaulted before the age of 16, and there are currently about 7.5 billion people on the planet, and roughly 5.6 billion of those people are over the age of 16, that means there are roughly one billion one hundred and twenty-five million adult survivors of sexual violence living, working and walking among us, give or take a few million. If we were talking about a virus, it would be an unimaginable pandemic. These are realities that people don't want to look at, and in looking away we diminish the importance. It's a pandemic of harm that goes unaddressed.

The kind of things that happened to me and my friends at CTC all those years ago are still happening today. I've had mothers reach out to me for advice on what to do about it. It's happening in theaters and education programs across town, and across the globe. The recent documentary, *Quiet on the Set,* about abuse at the Nickelodeon Network, is a perfect example of predatory behavior from people who are supposed to be protecting children in the arts.

Wherever kids are present, it's likely some form of abuse is happening by an employee, because where children go, so do those that would take advantage of them. It's how it works, and everyone running these institutions needs to shift their thinking to include taking

---

[40] Sometimes the media gets it right.

care of the human beings that have been harmed, and stop putting institutions ahead of the people.

Dismantling Rape Culture strongly depends on understanding the core reason it continues to thrive: The almighty Dollar. People put money above human beings. They do it in education, sports, arts, medicine, military, religious institutions, and the corporate world. Rape Culture survives in part because of the unwillingness of some people in charge to put the priority of human beings above their bottom line.

Questions to ask yourself before moving on:

- Did I hear anything in this chapter I hadn't heard before, or have I gained new awareness around something?
- How do I perpetuate the social contracts that were handed down to me?
- What kind of messages are being sent in my community that support Rape Culture?

Chapter Eight

The Truth about Sexual Violence

The prevalence of sexual violence in the world is a hard truth, an ugly reality that makes one want to disengage, binge-watch *The Great British Baking Show,* and sleep for a week. We don't want to hold that painful truth up to the light, the more we look at it the uglier it gets. But we *must* be willing to look at what's true before we can change it. Ignorance is not bliss, in this case, it's a free pass for people who perpetrate sexual crimes. We need to practice radical acceptance regarding the realities of Rape Culture and stop ignoring what's going on around us.

A few years ago, I was reading some of my old journals from when I was a teenager and came across an entry that gave me pause. I'd told my best friend about being assaulted when I was ten years old. I was surprised to read that I used the word "rape" in my written description of the conversation. I clearly knew what happened to me when I described it at age fifteen, but somewhere along the line, I'd stopped using the word "rape" to describe what happened to me long ago, even in my *thoughts.* On some level, I didn't want to accept the reality of what happened to me.

At a speaking engagement held shortly after the #MeToo movement took off, I heard a police officer talk about a moment that opened his eyes to the scope of the problem. He had asked a group of women at a talk he was giving to self-identify if they'd experienced sexual violence. One woman asked if "sexual violence" included "sexual harassment." The officer hadn't thought about that before, but knowing that harassment is legally defined as a form of sexual violence, he said "yes." At this point, every single woman in the room raised her hand. Every single one.

The officer then described how he went home and found his wife in the yard talking to a female neighbor. He told them about the meeting, and when he asked them what they thought happened when he asked the women to raise their hands, his wife and their neighbor said in unison, "Everyone raised their hand." This was a moment of awakening for that officer and a powerful reminder of the scope of the problem.

Before going further, let's reflect on the layers of acceptance we face when having difficulty accepting something that feels unacceptable. The realities of Rape Culture and our participation in it are harsh— you may come across something that you don't want to accept as true about what's going on around you or your participation in it. Or maybe you already have come across something that isn't sitting comfortably for you. If this is the case, try the exercise I demonstrated on the layers of acceptance from Chapter Three to process what you are feeling. Here is the list of layers that keep us from accepting things we find unacceptable:

- Layer One- *Identify the upset- What do I find unacceptable?*
- Layer Two- *Accept the reality of the situation as true, without emotional attachment, remembering that I don't need to like something to accept it.*
- Layer Three- *Identify what emotions are attached to the situation.*
- Layer Four- *Honor those emotions- My feelings matter.*
- Layer Five- *What idea do I have to let go of to find acceptance?*
- Layer Six- *How can I reframe an idea that is holding me back from acceptance?*

Do you see how it can pertain to Rape Culture? Fully understanding Rape Culture is hard if you're avoiding acceptance of harsh realities. You may find it difficult without some conversation. If so, consider reaching out to your processing partner or someone you know to be embedded in these kinds of conversations to get perspective.

~ Acceptance- See What's True ~

One of the barriers to acceptance is a lack of understanding. To help you find clarity around this subject, the National Sexual Violence Resource Center defines Sexual Violence this way:

- Rape or sexual assault
- Child sexual assault and incest
- Intimate partner sexual assault
- Unwanted sexual contact/touching
- Sexual harassment
- Sexual exploitation
- Showing one's genitals or naked body to other(s) without consent
- Masturbating in public
- Watching someone in a private act without their knowledge or permission

My additions to this list are:

- Electronic or internet offenses, such as revenge porn
- Sending sexual images electronically without consent from the receiver
- Solicitation for sex from minors

Though some items on this list are commonly understood as sexual violence, other definitions are blurry for some people. Sexual violence can fall into blurred categories.

My brother had a paper route when he was a kid. He became very ill with a horrible cold and I agreed to do his paper route for him because he was so sick. I think I was eleven—most definitely pre-pubescent. I'd watched and helped my brother prepare the papers for delivery before and knew what to do. I went down to the paper shack and started prepping the papers and putting them into my brother's bag. Having a paper route was a very boyish thing to do, and I didn't know any girls who did this job. I was surrounded by boys a lot bigger than me—I was the only girl around. One of the older boys was razzing me, saying that I looked too weak to be able to carry a bag full of papers. He said, "She's too little, she doesn't even have tits yet." Then he reached over and grabbed my chest and gave me what we referred to as a "titty twister." It hurt! Everyone laughed. I finished folding the papers as quickly as possible, tears filling my eyes, and I ran out.

Even though we were kids, this is a form of sexual violence.

When I was seventeen, I was at a party at my brother's house. There was a guy there who I had a crush on for many years. We ended up in a room alone and he closed the door. I was not alarmed at first because I'd never had an encounter with him that caused me to fear him, he'd always been very nice. But in this circumstance, he approached me aggressively, trying to restrain me, reach under my clothes, and kiss me. Typically, when someone comes after me in a sexually threatening way I tend to freeze or appease. In a rare moment of self-agency, I went into fight mode and pushed him back. This made him angry, and he grabbed me violently. He had had quite a bit to drink, I had not. I was able to wiggle my way away from him and left the room.

Even though he didn't succeed in his attack, this is a form of sexual violence.

When I was about twelve or so, back in the late 70s, I was playing at my neighborhood park. It was getting dark and I was heading home, walking past a little building on the park grounds. Out of an alcove in the building, a man came out of the shadows with his zipper open, his penis hanging out of his pants. He started walking towards me. I was absolutely terrified and ran all the way home. I had always considered the park a safe place to be, it was like an extension of home. The park no longer felt safe.

Even though he never even touched me, this is a form of sexual violence.

And now, let us address the last item on the Resource Center's list—watching someone in a private act without their knowledge or permission. It seems like that act could be interpreted in a way that lets the offender off the hook, in that what-you-don't-know-can't-hurt-you sort of way.

A close friend of mine told me about a confession she heard from a co-worker. This man had worked at the CTC in the early 1980s, and he described a side event in the theater that didn't have anything to do with the show he was hired for. He said a bunch of pre-teenage boys were led out onto the stage and told to walk around. The kids believed they were doing what we refer to in theater as a costume parade, but they couldn't see anyone watching them. The former employee said the purpose of this parade was so a group of men, gathered "behind some sort of one-way window," could masturbate in the dark while watching the children walk around on stage. It upset this man so much that he never worked there again.

There's significant evidence going back to 1961 pointing to CTC Artistic Director John Clark Donahue's connection to child abuse images[41] and sex trafficking rings in Minnesota. Because of this, this story seems not only plausible but likely.

Based on the man's account, my mind goes immediately to the wall of windows at the back of the theater, where Donahue's office was located, overlooking the stage from the balcony seating. These windows had curtains which were typically drawn, so audience members couldn't look into the office. From that vantage point, Donahue could keep tabs on the shows by watching performances with the lights off in the office and the curtains open. We knew that this setup meant Donahue was likely watching the show, and we couldn't see him, but he could see us. Because of this physical arrangement, it's easy to picture a group of young boys in costumes being led out and told to walk around on the stage, and a bunch of men up in Donahue's office, watching them and masturbating in the dark.

Imagine that you just figured out you were one of those kids. How does that thought land in your body? Does it make your stomach knot up? Do you see that it's a form of violence? No? Then think

---

[41] AKA Child pornography

about this—if someone takes a swing at another person and they miss, the punch doesn't land, was the violence removed from the action of the punch? It's still violence even if it doesn't hit the mark.

Even if a person doesn't know their privacy is being violated, this is a form of sexual violence.

These stories aren't easy to hear, but we must listen. While heading an initiative to write the Minnesota Theater Education Standards, I was talking to an actor friend of mine who was part of the editing team. He knew my personal story of abuse and what I'd witnessed at CTC all those years ago. We were discussing how harm can happen to theater students in classrooms. During our conversation about harm in theater education, he said, "...and then there's what happened to you and your friends, and I don't even want to go *there*." And there's the rub. Here was someone who was committed to creating change in the education structure that would help countless students, and he didn't want to "go there." I don't blame him. It's ugly stuff. But to make change for the better, so harm will stop happening, we *have to* go there. We have to be willing to accept the reality of harm that's happening and speak the truth about it.

~ Why Victims Don't Disclose ~

There are many reasons a person may choose not to disclose sexual violence. It's important to remember that each person's experience is unique, and an identical circumstance can land completely differently in two different victim-survivors based on their life experience. Below are some baseline reasons, and there are a million variations on each. And, of course, the reasons are certainly not limited to this list.

Some Reasons for Staying Silent:

- No one will believe you- It's painful to disclose sexual violence, and victim-survivors feel a lot of shame. If no one is going to believe you anyway it feels easier, even safer, to just stay silent.

- Victim blaming- It's entirely possible you'll be blamed for your own rape by authorities, or even friends and family. Victim-survivors already have extraordinary levels of shame, and the possibility of also being blamed is unbearable.
- "Boys will be boys"- Social Contracts say that males are aggressive, so this behavior is expected and accepted as "normal." If the assailant was male, the victim-survivor might believe the rape was normal.
- "Sugar and Spice"- Girls are conditioned by social contracts to always be nice. Disclosure might get someone into trouble, and it's not nice to get someone in trouble.
- "Making Mountains out of Mole Hills"- Someone may think you're making a big deal out of nothing, overreacting, or making it up. We convince ourselves it "wasn't really that bad."
- Sexual Stimulation- When your genitals are touched you can get aroused simply because that's how our bodies are designed to respond to touch. It's possible to have an erection or orgasm while being raped. Victim-survivors may assume they wanted to be treated that way and not tell anyone.[42]
- Fear of being considered weak- This is especially true for males because they're conditioned by social contracts to believe they must always be strong, and if they aren't strong, they're a "sissy."
- Fear of being labeled as "gay"- If the victim-survivor is assaulted by the same sex and they are heterosexual they may fear this label if they disclose.
- Fear of being alone- the assailant may be a spouse or domestic partner and disclosing may mean they'll go away, which might feel worse than staying silent about the assault.
- Lack of resources or a safe place to go- A rapist might be a spouse, domestic partner, or roommate, and the victim-survi-

---

[42] It's important to acknowledge that this physical response doesn't mean you consented to be raped, it just means you're human and had a normal human reaction to touch.

vor is dependent on that person for food and shelter for themselves or their children. They feel trapped by that dependence.

- You consented at the beginning but changed your mind- If the nature of the touch changes from what was a comfortable "yes," the victim-survivor may feel responsible because they chose to be intimate.
- You just want to forget it ever happened- If you ignore it, the feelings might go away and you won't have to think about it.
- You're embarrassed- you don't want to admit to yourself, let alone another human being, that you were raped.
- You don't believe a crime was committed- You may not understand the definition of rape and don't think that's what happened.
- Coercion- This is especially true when the victim-survivor is a minor. Young children are easily manipulated to believe they're a willing participant in sexual assault. Pubescent children are vulnerable because their hormones are ramping up and they're easily taken advantage of because they're naturally sexually curious. Predators use this to convince a child they wanted the sexual activity. Adults who are inexperienced with sexual contact can also be coerced to believe the behavior is normal.
- Not understanding criminal statutory rape- Laws exist to protect children from predatory sexual behavior.[43] Most children don't understand how the laws are applied. They may be considered the age of consent with partners their age[44], but don't know that the age of consent changes if the abuser is an adult in a position of power, such as a teacher, coach, counselor, etc. They don't know a crime was committed.

There are more reasons for not disclosing than I can count, but hopefully, this gives you a glimpse into the thought process that can

---

[43] The prefrontal cortex isn't fully developed until around the age of twenty-five, so laws are in place to protect young people who can easily be manipulated and don't have full capacity to consent based on brain development.

[44] Laws regarding age of consent vary from state to state.

happen for victim-survivors. The reasons to stay silent aren't always logical to an observer, but they make sense in the mind of the victim-survivor. Never judge someone for not disclosing. It's a very personal journey.

~ What Consent Looks Like ~

Eight out of ten rapes are perpetrated by someone who the victim-survivor knows.[45] We like to think of rape as something that only happens to people who aren't careful, who walk alone at night on empty streets, who engage in "risky" behavior; This is far from the truth.

In 1987, Mary Koss, PhD, published the first national study about sexual assault among college students. The "Hidden Rape Victim," as described by Dr. Koss, doesn't, "report rape, seek services, or even identify themselves as rape victims." Her research shone a light on how prevalent sexual violence is, recognizing that victim-survivors often don't categorize what happened to them as "rape." If she asked, "Have you ever been raped," a victim-survivor might answer "No." If she asked the question with different wording, such as, "Have you ever had sex against your will," the person who said they were never raped might say "yes" to the rephrased question.

In a similar vein, during a training session on domestic violence with a focus on strangulation, the instructor described how a victim-survivor answered "no" to the question, "have you ever been strangled," but answered "yes" to "have you ever lost consciousness when he had his hands on your neck?"[46] Understanding the context or actual definition of a term is important. Not everyone categorizes things the same way.

---

[45] https://www.rainn.org/statistics/perpetrators-sexual-violence

[46] Incidentally, in that DV training, I was stunned by these strangulation statistics given by the nurse doing the training. From my notes of the training; 99% of perpetrators are men, only 3% of victims seek medical help. These were sad but not surprising statistics. This one really got me—the likelihood of homicide by strangulation from a domestic partner once they have attempted it is increased by 750% to 1000%. Not a typo.

Consent is an important thing to understand and discuss. Not everyone comprehends the distinctions of what it looks like and what it doesn't. Victim-survivors sometimes don't know what happened to them, all they know is it didn't feel good, or it was "wrong."

Perpetrators sometimes don't realize that they didn't have consent. While this should never be used as an excuse or let them off the hook for their actions, there may be times when a perpetrator might not have understood that what they were doing wasn't consensual. Understanding consent can be pivotal in some circumstances.

There's a great acronym that was created by Planned Parenthood which makes it a little easier to remember. It's called FRIES. It stands for Freely Given, Reversible, Informed, Enthusiastic, and Specific. Let's look at what each one does and doesn't mean.

Freely given means not coerced in any way. The person giving consent is in full control of their decisions and makes them without feeling obligated to do something they don't want to do. They aren't under the influence of drugs, or alcohol, mentally incapacitated, or pressured by someone until they finally say "yes."

Reversible means someone can change their mind. Sometimes a person may think they're willing to do something but when the time comes, they realize they aren't. Everyone has the right to change their mind at any moment. What was a "yes" one day might be a "no" the next. "Yes" doesn't mean "yes forever." If someone says "yes," but later changes their mind, you stop. It doesn't mean you keep going because they were okay two minutes ago.

Informed means everyone is clear about what they're saying "yes" to. Agreements are mutual and followable. You can't change or alter what you agree to because you get swept up in the moment.

Enthusiastic means you want to do what you're doing. "Maybe" isn't enthusiastic and doesn't equal "yes."

Specific means your agreement is about certain things, not all things. Saying "yes" to making out doesn't mean you're saying "yes" to sex.

In the entertainment industry, there's a different acronym that makes consent clear in a work setting, such as theater, film, television, and dance. The acronym is CRISP[47]. It stands for Considered, Reversible, Informed, Specific, and Participatory. Let's break these down.

Three of the words are the same—Reversible, Informed, and Specific—because they apply to both real-world scenarios and work situations. Example: Reversible means a performer can decide after a scene is rehearsed that they actually aren't comfortable with choreographed movements or actions and can request that it be changed to something they're more comfortable with. Informed means everyone involved is clear about what they're agreeing to do with the movement or contact. Specific means you stick to what has been choreographed and don't deviate from it.

"Freely Given" is tricky to translate to the industry because you're getting paid to do a job. If you say "no" you might lose the job. Money and professional reputations are involved. "Freely Given" is replaced with "Considered," which allows the performer to consider all aspects of what they're saying "yes" to and agreed upon boundaries for safety in the work.

And "Enthusiastic" is tricky too. Sometimes you're asked as a performer to stretch beyond what is comfortable— it's part of the job. Consent in a performance isn't always going to be enthusiastic, sometimes roles are challenging, and actors are nervous or uncertain, so "Enthusiastic" is replaced with "Participatory." A performer has full agency to decide what they're willing to do, it isn't handed down to them by a director, they're part of the creative team deciding how to tell this element of the story.

~ False Reporting ~

False accusations happen, but they are rare.[48] Statistically, about 5 percent of people who make an accusation of sexual violence aren't telling the truth, and that number includes accusations that are legally

---

[47] https://www.idcprofessionals.com/blog/defining-consent-from-fries-to-crisp
[48] Side note: Historically, I think it's important to acknowledge that many of the 6000+ lynchings since the Civil War were based on racially motivated false accusations of sexual misconduct.

considered unsubstantiated— this is not to say that the accuser is lying outright, but that the investigation is unable to prove guilt. Perpetrators throw false reporting out as a shield for their actions, but this is proving to be an increasingly unconvincing defense.

The abuse that happened to some of the students at CTC can seem implausible because it was so egregious. A former classmate who wasn't a victim of abuse told me that they didn't believe a certain person's story of abuse they suffered at CTC. They thought the person had made it up for attention. My response was something like this: To me, it doesn't matter whether or not the event happened the way it was described by her. *Something* happened to cause her so much pain. I have compassion for the suffering that she is experiencing, no matter what the source of her pain is.

I want to elaborate on this very controversial issue with a story that is close to me. My son, Tucker, was accused of inappropriate behavior by a girl at college. He told me that this young woman was upset about something and having a terrible day, and he had given her a hug to console her, which is a very typical response from him, he's a very compassionate guy and gives great hugs. Later, she started telling people that he had touched her inappropriately. He told me he had thought very hard about how his actions could have been interpreted as aggressive or abusive. He was worried that he would get in trouble at school for something he hadn't done. "Mom, all I did was give her a hug because I felt bad for her," he told me, "Why would she say this about me?"

I was terribly concerned for both of them; for Tucker because of his reputation and good standing at school, and for this girl because I knew in my gut that something bad had happened to her at some point and she was in pain—people don't feel that way for no reason. It turns out that this is something she had done before—he heard from several other guys that she had done the same thing to them, taken non-threatening physical contact from a male, and interpreted it as assault, accusing them of touching her inappropriately. A week later he heard that she accused yet another young man.

At the time I was not in the place I am today regarding advocating for victims of sexual violence. Had I been, I would have tried to get some help for her, but I was just relieved that my son didn't get in trouble for a serious offense he didn't commit. I never forgot about the young woman though, and I hope she got some help. My guess is she was suffering from untreated chronic or complex trauma, PTSD, and she was feeling like every touch from a male was an offense because of it.

We need to believe people when they say they've been harmed. There's no doubt in my mind that that young woman had been sexually assaulted at some point, but my son didn't do it to her. She felt harmed. Period. I believe her— AND my son didn't do anything wrong. The fact that he didn't do something considered harmful doesn't cancel the fact that it landed as a violation for her. He's not guilty of a crime, AND she felt harm. Both things are true, it's not an "either, or."

Men have concerns about false accusations. The #MeToo movement put the fear of God in a lot of men— they're afraid that every single thing they did in their entire lives would be in question. They fear that now women can ruin their lives, their jobs, and their reputations just because they flirted with someone at work. I have two things to say about that:

1) You *should* do some deep self-searching of how you have participated in your own life. You should feel the same depth of self-examination that my son did because of an innocent hug. Women have spent their lives dealing with the consequences of the disregard of their bodies by men. Take some time to look at your life and see who you have been. If you did something wrong, clean it up! Be accountable.

2) The men you have seen taken down weren't fired for no reason. Employers don't take the firing of someone lightly; they can be easily sued because of it. In fact, they take it a lot more seriously than they do an accusation of sexual violence. They take far more action and care to make sure they aren't wrongly firing someone than they do handling the person

who was violated, because legally the offender has more rights than the person who was violated. If you didn't do anything wrong, "innocent before proven guilty" is on your side.

~ Vulnerable Communities and Privilege~

People in vulnerable communities, (e.g., disabled, elderly, minorities, women, and children) are more likely to be victims of crimes. Those of us who live free of discrimination or physical and mental disabilities and have more tangible resources experience crimes at lesser rates. This is not an opinion, it's about numbers.

Thirty-nine percent of female rape victims are disabled.[49] Native American women are twice as likely as any other race to experience sexual violence. More than fifty percent of sexual contact between inmates and prison staff is non-consensual. The statistics of sexual violence and homicide perpetrated against Transgendered people are staggering, especially Black trans-women. [50]

People tend to fear what they don't understand, so if you aren't part of these communities or already have an understanding of these issues, educating yourself is critically important. There's no better way to understand an issue than learning from someone who is affected by it. But unless you have a close relationship with someone that lends itself to a deep and personal conversation, or it's part of your job to explore these issues in a diverse group, asking someone from a community you aren't a part of to explain the problems they face, that you don't understand, is putting the burden of your education on them. Do some work on your own.

To understand issues in the LGBTQ community, and the Transgender community in particular, I suggest visiting GLAAD.org to learn more. Decisions are being made around the country by legislators who have no real understanding of the lives of Transgender people. Their ignorance is literally putting lives at risk. This needs to

---

[49] https://www.cdc.gov/violenceprevention/sexualviolence/svandipv.html
[50] RAINN.org

stop. Please educate yourself so you can be an ally to this vulnerable community.

"Privilege" is another issue to be addressed, especially as it relates to social contracts and the BIPOC community. For many of us, the term "white privilege" has no immediate resonance. For me, the word "privilege" meant "better than," and I usually equated it to having money. When I first heard the term "white privilege," I was offended by the idea that I had it. I'm not rich and I don't hold the fact that I'm white-bodied over anyone, so I didn't think it applied to me. What I didn't understand was that "white privilege" doesn't equate to an insult. It's something that goes with the color of my skin, not my character.

Are you struggling to grasp this? Here's a parallel example that might help— I'm tall and move through the world differently than people who are shorter than me. People who are short must get assistance from another person or use a stool or something to get a box down from the high shelf. I don't need help, but I don't think of it as having "height privilege"— it's inherent—it just goes along with being tall. But the fact is, I do have the privilege of being able to reach high places with ease. I can use my height privilege to help a person in a wheelchair get the jar of pickles from the top shelf at the grocery store. I may not completely understand the frustrations and limitations of being in that wheelchair because I don't live that life, but I'm certainly not going to say "no" when I can help someone in need. That would make me a jerk.

"White privilege" is afforded to those of us with white bodies. We have it inherently. We move through the world differently than people of color. This isn't because white is better, it's because the social constructs and social contracts handed down over generations have equated "whiteness" as "better," which is erroneous. White privilege simply means we've been afforded an easier way of moving through society because our skin has less melanin.

If you're white and argue with the idea that BIPOC communities are struggling, or don't believe they continue to be oppressed and suffer crimes like sexual violence and police violence at higher rates than white-bodied people, may I suggest that you visit NAACP.org to learn more about what's happening in those communities.

If we continue to ignore the realities facing vulnerable communities, and not listen to them when they share their experiences and ask for our allyship, it's the same as ignoring the person in the wheelchair asking for help. Do you really want to be that person? Educate yourself and use your privilege to push against the social contracts that uphold oppressive social constructs.

It's important to believe survivors when they tell you they've been victimized. This is especially true for those in vulnerable communities. They've been ignored and told for centuries their experiences aren't real or don't matter. It's hard for anyone to disclose about abuses they've endured. When there's a social contract that says, "You matter less," it's even harder to let go of the shame that keeps victim-survivors silent. Use what privilege you have to lift up their stories to help them be seen.

Questions to ask yourself before moving on:

- Do I have a better understanding of sexual violence now?
- Is there something I'm resisting putting into that category?
- Do I need to talk to someone about anything that got stirred in me while reading?

Chapter Nine

Shifting the Culture

Rape Culture is an implicit or unconscious cultural agreement that allows perpetrators of sexual violence to harm people without consequences. None of us remembers ever agreeing to any contract that would allow such a thing. This is something that happened a long time ago and was passed on through the generations. Unfortunately, it continues to rule the way society responds to sexual violence and how it sees itself.

It's time that we renounce any participation in this contract. If there were a paper version, we could burn it. I guess that's what women were doing back in the 1970s when they were burning their bras—they were flipping the bird to that social contract.

If the language surrounding Rape Culture sounds reminiscent of the ways people talk about white privilege and white supremacy, that's because it's the same structure that holds these destructive models in place—they're used to exploit for profit and enforce patriarchal ideals. I'm drawing a parallel to illustrate the importance of dismantling both. It's up to each of us to shine the healing light of truth on these wounds of our society. We need to educate ourselves, and each other, to stand together and not shy away from the ugly truths. It's the only way to take down these hardened structures once and for all. The power of our collective voices is undeniable.

Allow me to take a moment to reach out to my Black and Brown-bodied female friends, all of those glorious BIPOC women who have endured the double jeopardy of these power structures. I see you. I love you. I believe you'll change the world. You are inspiring.

~ Action- Creating a Culture of Consent ~

We need to be willing to replace Rape Culture with Consent Culture in every area of our lives. We should stop in our tracks when we see that something is wrong and not uphold a system that relies on willful ignorance, even if it means inconveniencing ourselves—even if it means we walk away from something we've invested time and money in. Here are a few things that keep us from doing that:

- We don't want to accept how prevalent sexual violence is, largely because people don't want to talk about it or look at it because it's so ugly.
- We don't want to see that we allow this problem to flourish by ignoring it, which emboldens those who perpetrate the crimes because they know they can get away with it.
- We think it's not our problem to solve.
- We think the problem is unsolvable.
- We believe that victims of sexual violence are partly responsible for what happens to them.

It's hard to find the balance in this truth-telling. People become overwhelmed by it after a while. Conversations about racial divisions in this country can be exhausting and frustrating. "Can we please talk about something else?" Yes... and no. Yes, because people do need to take a break from the intensity—self-care is important. And no, because it isn't going to change unless we stay present to the truth and focused on change. Change doesn't happen by wishing something away, it happens through hard work and persistence.

How do we combat something so prevalent in our society? We speak the truth. We name it. We make space for others to speak their truth, and we listen. We encourage those who are afraid. We allow one voice to become ten, to become a hundred, to become a thousand until the chorus of voices is so loud it can't be denied.

On January 21, 2017, the largest single-day protest in US history took place. People joined The Women's March across the country, (and in other countries as well) to peacefully protest the inauguration of Donald Trump. Singer Annie Lenox memorably responded when asked by a reporter about Donald Trump's comment about grabbing women by the "pussy," calling it, "a catalyst to wake women up." And it wasn't just women who rose up that day, it was all kinds of people.

In 2016, California Superior Court Judge Aaron Persky sentenced twenty-year-old student Brock Turner for sexually assaulting Chanel Miller outside a fraternity. Miller was on the ground, unconscious, and Turner's assault on her was stopped by two passersby. Though Turner was convicted of felony sexual assault, Judge Persky gave Turner a lenient sentence of just six months in county jail, not prison, followed by three years of probation. He reasoned that because Turner was drunk when he raped Miller, and had no "significant record of prior criminal offenses," there was "less moral culpability attached to the defendant," and that, "a prison sentence would have a severe impact on him."[51] Miller's life was forever changed by being raped by Turner, but the judge seemed to think that Turner showed great promise and his actions weren't bad enough to forever change *Turner's* life by putting him in prison.

Rape Culture is part of what allowed Judge Persky to give Turner such a lenient sentence for felony rape. Allow me also to shine a light on the fact that Miller is of Asian descent, and Turner is White. I wonder aloud: Persky's decision essentially ignored the impact of Miller's trauma by showing great lenience for her attacker— would his decision have been different if she looked more like him? Would Turner's sentence have been more severe if he were a young man with great promise, but Black? I'll just set that there and move on...

Here's some good news— California voters re-called Judge Persky for his actions. This is what it looks like to commit to a new social contract. One that doesn't blame victims of sexual violence for crimes committed against them, that respects the dignity of someone who has been harmed at the core of their humanity. This is an example

---

[51] The full text Persky's decision was published in The Guardian https://www. theguardian.com/us-news/2016/jun/14/stanford-sexual-assault-read-sentence-judge-aaron-persky

of "change the things we can." People reacted with outrage, but they took action, they engaged in a response.

In Chapter Two we discussed reaction versus response. Hopefully, you learned to recognize the difference between when you act on impulse and when you have agency in the choices you make. You can take that understanding and apply it to a broader context, from how to shift your mind away from negative thoughts and use it to engage with the cultural shift to dismantle Rape Culture.

~ Breaking the Silence ~

One of the first action steps we can take to shift the culture is to break the silence around sexual violence. Rape is one of those words people don't like to say out loud, like the word "cancer" forty years ago. It required hushed voices to discuss it. Now, we run marathons in the name of cancer research and survivors. We need to make it okay for people to discuss sexual violence.

The following is from my memoir, *Shattered*. It's a straightforward description of what it means for victim-survivors of sexual violence to break their silence around their abuse:

"Breaking the Silence means speaking truth about sexual violence. It means speaking truth to power, saying what's true even if you're scared. It means not allowing fear to stop you from having a voice or allowing things that should be spoken to go unsaid. It means not suffering in silence and throwing down the shackles of shame that keep you tethered to it. It doesn't require a monumental, courageous act. It can be telling one person something that's painful, and you've kept to yourself or feared what might happen if you said it out loud. It means honoring your own narrative."

You don't have to have been assaulted yourself to be able to talk articulately about shifting the culture. We can all make efforts to normalize the conversation. Lean into it when it comes up. Yes, it's a subject that can make it feel like the air is being sucked out of the room. There are certainly better times than others to have deep conversations about it. The point is we need to stop treating it like a taboo subject. It's in conversation that we learn and grow as a society. Make the commitment to educate yourself about this subject so that if it comes up you have something to say to further the efforts to shift away from Rape Culture and towards a Culture of Consent.

I used to volunteer at the women's prison in Shakopee Minnesota. Every volunteer had to go through yearly training at the prison. There are a variety of different kinds of groups that donate their time, from church groups to theater-makers. The training is the same for everyone, consisting of basic information about protocols to be followed. One of the trainings I attended included several older retirees from what I assume was a church group, many of them knew each other.

Checking into the prison was a multi-step process, and only a few people were allowed through the entry point at a time. One small group would go through, then wait for the rest. There were about twenty of us there for the training, mostly women, and I was in one of the first groups to go through. I was standing on one side of the hallway waiting for the others, and the only two men in attendance were standing across from me on the opposite wall. A few more people came through, and one of the women came over to one of the men and playfully smacked him on the arm—I'm assuming they were married.

"You didn't wait for me," she said, hitting him lightly.

"Ouch!" he said melodramatically, "Sexual harassment, sexual harassment!"

He and the man standing next to him began to laugh. "You better be careful," the other man said, "don't defend yourself. She might come back thirty years from now saying you sexually harassed *her*." The two men laughed and laughed.

This was not long after the wave of #MeToo stories brought the social reckoning of sexual harassment front and center in the media. I looked around the hallway at the dozen or so other women standing there with me. No one was laughing. We were all looking down at the ground or looking around at each other with stunned faces. No one said anything. I was tongue-tied. I wish I'd said something, but I couldn't find the words.

Driving home later, I thought about what I could have said. "I don't mean to interrupt, but I'd like to point out that statistically one in four women have experienced sexual violence in their lives, so of the twelve women standing here, three of us are survivors. I hope you'll consider that next time you choose to make jokes about sexual violence against women."

That's what I wanted to say, but even my carefully thought-out rebuke is problematic. My Minnesota Nice[52] upbringing is ingrained in me, and that social contract, combined with my False Core Beliefs, tells me that I have no place telling a man how he should talk, or interrupt their fun. This unspoken response is colored with apologies for speaking the truth, even in my own *thoughts*.

Abiding by the social contract of silence after my rapes felt like a given. I knew how rape victims were treated; often they weren't believed, and if they were they were blamed for what happened to them. I felt partially responsible for what happened to me—I didn't scream or try to beat my offenders off of me. From the outside, it could have looked like I wanted to be treated that way or consented to it.

I wish that I'd been able to break my silence sooner. The truth is I wasn't ready. I needed to shed a lot of fear and shame to do it. I needed to accept the reality of what happened before I was able to find my voice. Once I found it, I was compelled to use it.

For me, choosing to go public about my rapist was liberating, but also terrifying. Not only because I wasn't sure how people would see me, but I was scared my rapist would try and sue me for slander. When I asked my lawyer what would happen if he did, he said, "Let 'em try, the truth is on your side."

Breaking the Silence publicly isn't the answer for everyone, and it doesn't come without risks. There are things to consider. You can't just say whatever you want and expect no repercussions. You need to

---

[52] Minnesota nice is a cultural stereotype applied to the behavior of people from the Midwest, implying residents are unusually courteous, reserved, mild-mannered and passive-aggressive. Wikipedia

get clear about what you're doing, and how to do it, and be prepared for backlash. You have to be willing to stand up to forces that want to knock you down. I'd suggest talking to a lawyer first, so that you completely understand what might happen and what your legal rights are.[53]

~ Hold the Line of Personal Space ~

There's an invisible circle that surrounds every person, a boundary of personal space that exists which should be respected. Generally, it lives at about a three-foot distance from our body, or arm's length. Many people spent a lot of time thinking about personal space during the pandemic. The six foot rule of social distancing in populated spaces gives us a tangible reference to this invisible line. It's where our personal spaces bump up against each other— the line you shouldn't cross unless you're invited to.

When someone we know and are comfortable with steps over that border, it can feel great. Sharing the energy of that space with someone we like is usually a good thing. But if someone unwelcome enters our space it's incredibly uncomfortable. We learn to accept the invasion in certain circumstances, like riding a bus, walking in a crowd, or sitting in a theater. We know we have to allow that line to be crossed because of the situation.

When men don't respect a woman's personal space, women tend to move the boundary instead of insisting that the line be honored. If someone sits too close to us, we try to inch away from the invader to increase the distance between us, not ask *them* to move. This may not be true everywhere or in every community, but it's definitely the way it is in Minnesota. Our "Minnesota Nice" upbringing is ingrained in us, and it's powerful programming that supersedes our instinct to hold that line. It doesn't feel natural for me to hold that line because the invasion of personal space has been normalized by my culture, and because most men don't think about it.

---

[53] Free legal advice is available at www.LawHelp.org

Several years ago, I was in a bar and there was a very drunk man there who was clearly bothering people. My companion went to the bathroom, leaving me alone at the bar, and this guy stumbled over, invading my space and aggressively hitting on me. I was looking over at the bartender, hoping he would intervene, but he didn't. Instead of telling him to back off, I went into my freeze /appease mode, trying to adjust myself so he wouldn't be touching me. When the person I was with came back, they sat down and the guy backed off, but he didn't completely leave me alone. My companion liked being at this bar and seemed to ignore my discomfort. I sat there trying not to make a fuss so as not to disrupt the good time my friend was having. I cut the evening very short and left. There are so many things wrong with this: 1) My own silence and dismissal of my personal space by not insisting he back off. 2) A bystander that wouldn't help. 3) My companion ignoring my discomfort.

I like to think that if this were to happen today, the outcome would be very different because I've learned to have agency in my choices around my own body, to hold safe boundaries, and to speak the truth. I'm exercising a new muscle.

It's normal for women and other marginalized groups to just move the line and deal with the discomfort— we learn to do this at a young age. But the #MeToo movement seems to be bringing awareness to men as never before. They're starting to look at their own participation in issues like this, which never registered to them as a big deal. Now that women have spoken up en masse, men are seeing actions they've been doing their whole lives in a different light, more aware now of how it lands for the person whose space is being invaded. Gen Z and Millennials seem to be better at holding the line because it's more acceptable for their generation to say, "Back off bub!" They provide a good role model for an older gal like me, who has spent her life moving the boundary.

It's time to hold the line! Recognize you have the RIGHT to take up space and hold your boundaries. Stop allowing people to invade your space without permission. You don't need to be mean about it, just firm. If someone says, "What's the big deal?" you can say something like, "It may not be a big deal to you, but that doesn't mean it's not important to me. I'll thank you for respecting my space."

If you're one of those people who hasn't been aware of how close you stand to others or who repeatedly disregards that line, knock it off. Pay attention. Ask permission. If someone holds that line at a time that seems weird, don't judge, just honor it and don't take it personally. Not everything is about you.

If you recognize that you didn't hold the line, or you didn't honor someone else's, go back later and acknowledge it if possible. It's amazing how something, that can seem so small, can make a huge difference in how safe you feel.

One more thing; "No" is a complete sentence. It needs no explanation.

~ Empower the Bystander ~

Breaking the silence doesn't just mean speaking out about something that happened to you, it also means calling attention to a problem when you see it. To name it and not shy away from the conversation. When we see things happen that don't sit right with us, we need to say something about it, clearly and directly. Expecting people to simply stop exhibiting poor behavior because times are changing is unrealistic. Gentle requests to be more respectful can often go unheard. Getting loud can get people's attention, but it can also put them into a defensive mode, making them stop listening, so no matter how loud you are, they won't hear you. So, what the heck *do* we do? We *be* the example.

When you're out in the world, pay attention to what's going on around you. Listen to people when they say something isn't right. Read body language. Use your voice. Show up in uncomfortable conversations you want to avoid and have them anyway. Speak when you see something is wrong and don't let fear rob you of your "better angels."

If you see someone being harassed, ask them, "Are you okay? Do you need help?" But don't assume that someone who is being bothered wants your help, or just barrel in and take over. You remove that person's agency over their own choices by taking over. Offer help by asking if they want it. If they say "no," then step aside, but don't necessarily go away. Things can happen fast; your bystander privilege might need to be invoked.

If you miss an opportunity to speak out against harm because you freeze, or because there isn't an opportunity to address something in the moment, you can go back later. Here's some language you could use to address something you didn't speak up about:

Can we talk about what happened the other day?...
I'm not sure if you're aware of this, but...
I'm not okay with what happened...
I see you acting in ways that don't fit with who I know you to be...

~ Empowering Children ~

Raising children is hard. Parents and guardians of young kids have a difficult task keeping them safe because kids are curious, and pushing the lines of safety is part of learning. Sometimes you have to grab them by the collar and whisk them out of the way of a speeding car to keep them from getting run over. But there's a time and place for everything. I believe the best thing we can do for our children is to instill in them a sense of agency over their own bodies. Period. It *will* transform the culture.

We need to stop making children sit on Santa's lap if they don't want to. Is a photograph more important than your child's sense of safety? It's not okay to force kids to go kiss their Auntie or spend time with your creepy cousin Charlie just because you don't want to offend a family member. Children _must_ have a say in what happens to them or they will be at risk of harm from people who would take advantage of their inability to hold their own safe space. I can't stress this enough.

Having experienced a very real and dangerous environment where I was harmed by an adult, and grownups took advantage of kids all around me, I had a strong commitment to make sure my kids knew very early on that they had the ultimate say over their bodies.

We need to teach our children to respect their own boundaries and the boundaries of others by modeling that behavior with them and others. They're always watching us. Actively teach them with love and compassion, especially when they do something wrong—which they will.

Around the age of four, one night while I was tucking him in, my son Calvin told me that he didn't want me to kiss him goodnight anymore. I was taken aback at first. *What do you mean you don't want me to kiss you, I'm your MOM!* I decided that I wasn't going to take it personally and decided to find out why. "I just don't like it when you get so close to my face," he said.

About a year earlier, a little boy at Calvin's daycare center bit him several times, leaving teeth marks all over his face. It was traumatic as a mom to see the results of what this little jerk had done to my child, and traumatic for my son to be the one receiving the bites, so I knew there was physical trauma he was still processing. He was unable to connect those dots rationally, but his *body* remembered it. All he knew, with his limited ability to understand, was that he didn't like my face coming at his face. I told him that I loved him and I wouldn't kiss him goodnight anymore but asked if it was okay to hug him. He looked relieved and agreed, because he wanted affection from me, but it needed to fit with his need to feel safe too. It was a solution we were both comfortable with, and eventually, it stopped being an issue, in his time, not mine.

When Tucker was twelve, he went away to a week-long summer camp for the first time. I was terrified that something might happen to him, that he would be hurt by an adult or another camper. I didn't want to freak him out and make him uncomfortable at camp, worrying about what might happen to him the whole time, but I wanted him to know that he was in charge of himself. I'd always made sure my kids understood about strangers, that even though they may be friendly they aren't your friends. I decided it was time to go a step further. We talked about autonomy and self-agency.

I told him that not everyone in the world has his best interest at heart. Some people tell kids things that aren't true to get them to do things they aren't comfortable doing (I didn't go into details; I kept it age-appropriate). I told him that he didn't need to do anything asked of him that didn't feel right. I told him that if anyone ever told him not to tell me something because they would hurt him or his parents if he did, he should tell me anyway, no matter what that person said. "Sometimes people lie about bad things they do to keep from getting into trouble, and they threaten others to stay quiet. You don't need to let them know you know this, just agree to keep quiet and then tell me or your dad right away anyway." He understood my serious tone, but I kept it straightforward and low-key emotionally because I didn't want to project my fear of what might happen to him. He appreciated my parental advice and empowerment of his autonomy, and I felt better knowing he had clear instructions on what to do in case anyone tried to silence him. He went off to camp and had a great time and went back again the following summer.

When Calvin was around twelve, he had terrible pain in his knees. He was growing at the time, as kids do when you feed them, so it was likely growing pains, but they were excessive— he was having trouble walking up and down stairs. I decided to take him to the doctor to discuss it. His pediatrician wanted to check for Lyme disease, to rule it out. The test requires a blood draw from the arm.

No kid that I know of likes to have blood taken, and Calvin was already not a fan of a finger prick. When he found out that it was going to be a needle in his arm, he went into a panic. He had never had to do it before and was terrified. Having had similar responses to needles when I was a child, I knew how it felt to be poked and prodded and feel helpless. I'd always given my children agency in deciding how they move through the world, and I wasn't going to stop then. I spent twenty-five minutes with him, explaining why the test was important, talking about what it would be like, that I had to have similar tests when I was young, that I wouldn't leave his side, and I'd hold his hand and let him squeeze it as hard as he could while they did it.

He decided to allow it, but as soon as they got the needle in his arm he panicked and pulled his arm away, which was painful and messy. I took another twenty minutes to help him calm down and try again. I could tell the technician was getting impatient, but I wasn't going to force him or hold him down. I was going to make sure he was in full agreement with this bodily invasion and ignored the sighs from the lab tech. Eventually, they got the blood they needed and I took Calvin to get ice cream as a reward.

When we got home, he could barely walk from the pain, so I told him I'd give him a piggyback ride down the stairs. "But mom, what about your back?" he said, concerned for my ongoing back issues. I thanked him for thinking about my well-being, assured him I'd be fine for a short jaunt, and set him down on the couch. After getting him settled, I looked at him and he had big tears welling up in his eyes. Concerned that I'd hurt him I asked, "What is it, buddy?" He said, "You're like, *sniffle*, *Super Mom*." It was one of the best moments in my parenting life. I'd honored my son's right to make decisions about his own body, and he knew it, and I'd modeled my own agency showing him I knew my own personal limits and didn't needlessly put myself at risk. [54]

Several years ago, a friend shared with me about her five-year-old being asked by his pediatrician if she could touch him during his physical. I was impressed. I'd never heard of a Dr. asking a child's permission to touch them. Since then, I've heard other such stories and am glad it's becoming a trend.

~ Institutional Accountability: Putting People First ~

Accountability can feel like a four-letter word. Who took the cookie from the cookie Jar? *Not me!* When did we learn that being accountable for our actions was a bad thing?

---

[54] Thankfully, he did not have Lyme Disease.

accountability[55]
noun
: *an obligation or willingness to accept responsibility or to account for one's actions*

In some Indigenous cultures, when someone does something wrong, that person is put into the middle of a circle and the community gathers around them. With care, the community shares things about the person in the middle. Not bad things, not ridicule for their faults, they reflect the good in that person, so they can see that part of themselves amplified through the voices of people who care about them. To bring them back to their better selves. What a beautiful notion. Wouldn't you be more likely to walk toward accountability and not away from it if that's how you would be held when you falter?

As more is revealed about the harm that has been occurring for decades at organizations in all arenas and career fields, we must insist that businesses and educational institutions adopt new policies and acknowledge the experience of the victim-survivor— they need to walk towards accountability, not away from it. It's Rape Culture that holds current harmful practices and policies in place, and if we want to take care of those that have been harmed, we need to dismantle it.

In CTC's case, lawyerly intrusion seemed to be coloring their actions throughout the process. This makes sense in some respect because not only did CTC have a team of lawyers battling for them, but their board of directors was filled with lawyers. This is typical of nonprofit organizations. Perhaps if they'd had artists on their board, their decisions would have been different, and more humane. This doesn't tend to be the case, however, because large organizations have large boards that require a fiduciary contribution to be made as part of their bylaws. Most artists I know don't have thousands of dollars sitting around. This represents gatekeeping at its finest: keep the "have-nots" out of the spaces where the "haves" are in power.

Having boards that can validate the experience of survivors of

---

[55] Merriam-Webster.com

harassment and sexual violence can transform them, but it isn't enough to just say, "We believe you." They need to recognize that the institution's prior silence allowed their organization to continue, to thrive even, at the cost of the survivor's mental health and well-being.

CTC had an opportunity to be an example of how to do it right. Instead, their behavior remains indicative of the overall viewpoint of most long-term businesses, organizations, and institutions: they believe that their history doesn't matter.

Here's the truth: harm happens everywhere. If you have human beings working for your company, at some point in time at least one of those humans in a position of power has sexually harassed or abused another person with less power within the institution. In the slim chance that no one has, the possibility for it to happen in the future is 100%, no matter what kind of policies and practices you have in place. We must stop thinking about sexual violence as something that happens everywhere except for where *we* are.

When we see the fallibility of our heroes, whether they be a person or a beloved institution, it psychologically pushes against us in uncomfortable ways. Some people didn't like that CTC was called out for their disregard for victim-survivors, or their other missteps. These willfully uninformed individuals chose to believe that the institution wasn't at fault. They were angry and didn't want to question their own happy experience or that of their children. *A place that makes such beautiful art couldn't possibly be at fault.* Yes, actually, it can. Multiple truths are absolutely possible. And one doesn't cancel out the other.

Public cries for accountability from beloved institutions are often met with hostility from people whose experience differs from those calling for justice. They don't understand why others don't see the value in the place or person being called out. Here's the thing: something can be good and harmful at the same time. This is a difficult concept to embrace. People like clear answers. It's much more calming to our systems when we can compartmentalize and don't have to question. It can be exhausting to be in an ambiguous place. We go for black-and-white thinking because it's easy.

Is institutional harm possible to change? Despite the many missteps we've witnessed, there are nonetheless some encouraging signs. But it'll take more than a glimmer of awareness and empathy on the part of leaders to achieve it. Organizations must be willing to put the well-being of human beings ahead of their bottom lines. Policy changes can't just be performative; they must have the commitment and follow through that speaks to the human element of the equation, or their efforts will fall flat.

For those who are focused primarily on numbers, putting employee well-being first seems counterintuitive, but there are many documented successes. I watched my ex-husband keep his theater company going through the 2009 recession while many other theaters dropped like flies. By deciding to put the people who worked for him ahead of his own interests, his company survived. You build loyalty when you treat people with respect and dignity, and money can't buy that.

If you're a leader in the thick of it and want to truly make a difference in the lives of the people who have been harmed at the institution you're running, get advice from a place like The Center for Institutional Courage. A company's lawyers will present a very specific lens through which to see the issues. It's their job. But that is only one part of the equation. Stop listening solely to your lawyers and let your heart speak to you.

~ Ten Things You Can Do Right Now ~

There's no way we're going to get to the other side of Rape Culture without making mistakes. People will get hurt. Wrong words will be spoken. When it happens to you, because it will, be accountable for your actions. Recognize the fallibility of our humanness. Give yourself and others permission to stumble and fall. Create space and opportunity for accountability. But don't do it at the cost of your well-being.

Here are ten things you can do right now to help dismantle Rape Culture:

1. **Say what's true.**

   Exercise your truth-speaking muscles by practicing speaking truth in every area of your life, especially *good* truth. Speaking truth gets easier the more you do it. Tell people you admire how awesome they are and do it often. Before you know it, you'll be an expert truth-teller.

2. **Believe people.**

   When someone says they were harmed, believe them without justification. It doesn't matter what the circumstances were, your default should be to believe them. And don't do it quietly, say the words—*I believe you.*

3. **Hold the line.**

   If someone gets in your personal space without permission, hold your boundary line and ask them to back off. You have the right to do this, it's *your body.* You can be polite but be firm.

4. **Empower children.**

   Our children need to have agency over their own bodies. Ask permission to touch them. Help them understand they have a say in who touches them, and teach them to respect the boundaries of others. Provide them with healthy, consent-based, age-appropriate information about sex education. Arm them with knowledge so they can make healthy choices in relationships and in the media they consume.

5. **Name Rape Culture when you see it.**

   Be an advocate for change. When you hear things that uphold Rape Culture, like rape jokes or derogatory terms for women and other underrepresented people, name it.

6. **Don't just be a bystander, be an active upstander.**

   When you see someone saying or doing something that isn't okay with you, say so.

7. **Be accountable.**

   When you do something wrong—and you will—be accountable for it. If you can't find the words in the moment, you can always go back later and make it right.

8. **Demand institutional accountability.**
   Don't allow employers to get away with not addressing power dynamics that uphold Rape Culture in their businesses. If they don't make strides toward change, take your business elsewhere.

9. **Stop putting money toward upholding Rape Culture.**
   You have a choice about the movies you see, the theaters you patronize, the music you listen to, the news you watch. Stop supporting social narratives that continue to uphold Rape Culture. Seek out artists, media, and movements that are committed to shifting the culture and support them with your time and money.

10. **Be a model of change.**
    Encourage others by being a model. You never know who is watching you. BE LOUD.

Advocating for ourselves and others is a scary affair. It's time to be courageous, walk forward despite our fear, and stop allowing it to keep us from doing what's right. When we take our fear by the hand and stay in motion, amazing things happen.

I don't like the word "fearless" when it comes to this work. Fearless is for gladiators and race car drivers. Courage is the stuff of advocates and survivors, those who walk consistently forward, not knowing how it'll turn out, yet doing it because it's the next right thing to do. Courage has many faces. Sometimes it looks like testifying in a courtroom. Sometimes it looks like stepping in harm's way to advocate for the needs of someone unable to do it for themselves. It can also look like picking up the phone to ask for help when you're struggling. It's the same thing, and it all counts.

Walking forward in the face of fear causes us to become bigger than we were, to stretch beyond our boundaries, and to find things we didn't know existed. Yes, sometimes the things we find in that unknown territory aren't so great. More often than not, though, we can find something beautiful we didn't even know we needed. If we only pursue the things that are known to us, we'll never grow.

Epilogue

For me, there is great resonance in the saying "The way out is through." It's been my experience. Honoring my body and listening to my inner voice have been critical to my healing process.

Growing beyond trauma requires a thorough investigation. It's like taking a puzzle apart and examining all the pieces before putting it back together. Sometimes we need to allow ourselves to go to emotionally uncomfortable places. This examination of our internal landscape can be overwhelming, which is why accompaniment in our healing process is so important— it requires emotional safety and control. When we give ourselves over to the process of healing trauma, we also need to know when to pull ourselves back. So, I want to leave you with my thoughts on boundaries— external and internal.

Keeping ourselves physically and emotionally safe requires boundaries, and figuring out what those boundaries are can be challenging. It can take time and require the support of others. Once we know what they are, it can be even more difficult to hold them. As with most change, it doesn't happen overnight. And holding boundaries takes practice.

Physical boundaries are probably the easiest to understand but can still be difficult to hold. A "No Trespassing" sign is pretty clear— don't go there! A verbal warning of "don't touch me" doesn't require an explanation. But how do you hold a physical boundary when someone doesn't want to respect it?

Safety is at the center of this question for me, both physical and emotional. If there is a real physical threat, you have every right to protect yourself, so do what you need to— yell, hit, scream, whatever.

Physical boundaries not being honored can make us feel unsafe emotionally too. Maybe there is no imminent danger, but that doesn't mean you don't have the right to ask that your physical boundary be honored.

When I was being bothered by that guy in the bar, I didn't hold my physical boundaries. I froze. Here are some things I would say today in the same circumstance— feel free to use them yourself if you find the need.

- I need you to take two steps away from me, right now.
- I didn't ask you to come that close, back off.
- It doesn't matter why; you just need to do it.

Some people aren't physically safe in their own homes. Setting a physical boundary might actually put one in more danger. If this is you, I encourage you to get help. No one deserves to be treated poorly, no matter what you may have done.

Emotional boundaries are harder to figure out. To help you figure out what yours are, here are some universal truths I know to be true:

- No one deserves to be treated poorly.
- We all have the right to be happy.
- We don't have to accept unacceptable behavior from others.

You may not believe these are true for everyone, but trust me, they are.

Something that upsets you may be no problem for someone else, so your boundaries will be unique to your situation and life experiences. You need to figure out where those lines are for yourself.

Very different from physical boundaries, holding emotional boundaries can be extremely difficult. Old patterns are hard to break. And the people in our lives can make it even harder, especially those closest to us. They're used to us being a certain way. Sometimes, they don't want us to change, but that doesn't mean we can't or shouldn't.

Not allowing someone to treat me disrespectfully is me holding an emotional boundary. And I don't need to explain myself when I hold that boundary— I may choose to, but I don't have to. The validity of my boundary is *not* contingent on the understanding of others. Here are some words you can use to stop someone in their tracks when they aren't honoring your emotional boundaries:

- I'm not okay with what just happened.
- You don't get to speak to me like that.
- I need you to stop doing what you're doing.
- I'm going to walk away and I ask that you not follow me.

I still get flustered when people are rude to me, and I hate confrontation. I avoid it whenever I can. Here are some less pointed "go-to" words that can give me time to collect myself if I'm triggered.

- I need to take a minute.
- You may be right, I need to think about that.
- I don't have the words right now. Maybe I will later.

I recommend writing down some responses you might use in your unique situation and practicing them so you have them ready. As with any new skill, practicing something like holding boundaries is important. Having a plan isn't enough; you need to practice saying the words out loud.

Internal boundaries are another thing altogether, and also very personal to the individual.

When trauma healing happens, parts of us that have long been silent are given a voice, and they may have a lot to say! Once acknowledged, those parts can be hard to quiet down. Holding internal boundaries can help you stay centered— without them, we can get stuck in the story of what happened and not focus on the healing process.

I can't tell you what your internal boundaries should be, but I can give you an example of how I hold one of mine.

When I was a small child, I was sitting on the kitchen floor playing with a glass bottle of tonic water, shaking it up. I dropped it and it exploded, sending shards of glass everywhere, including my face.

I was too young to cognitively remember this event, but I have scars on my face— and my body still holds the energy of the physical and emotional trauma of it.

Before I processed this trauma, anytime anything unexpected would come at my face, like someone playfully splashing water at me in a pool, I would start shaking, burst into a fit of tears, and hyperventilate. Even as an adult, I would no longer be in control. It made no sense. There was no danger, yet my body reacted as if there were.

Through conversations with my mother— she was the one who witnessed the bottle explode— I figured out that my oversized reaction to things coming at my face had that specific genesis. Since that revelation, I no longer get triggered in the same way. My body will still react, and probably always will, but because I have an adult understanding of that childhood event and I've processed that trauma, I can make a conscious choice about how to respond to something flying in my face. I can acknowledge the little Laura who gets scared and wants to cry. I might even let her, depending on the circumstance, but I hold a loving internal boundary with that part of myself, and I don't allow her to take the wheel— I stay in control; I don't need a two-year-old in the driver's seat of my life.

One might think of holding internal boundaries as compartmentalizing, but I don't like that term. It implies closing something off emotionally or shutting it down, which is very different from holding a healthy boundary. I spent decades of my life burying uncomfortable feelings because it was easier to be numb. I'm not suggesting you shut any part of yourself down, but there are better or safer times than others to allow the wounded parts of yourself to be in the driver's seat. Think of it as hitting a pause button— you can go back to the issue or emotion if needed at an appropriate time.

If you have trouble figuring out what your internal boundaries should be, I suggest you look at your False Core Beliefs— the boundaries will be next to them. When you tell yourself the truth about those false beliefs, the boundaries become clear.

I didn't become competent at holding boundaries until recently. And I still stumble. There are days when my inner demons get the best of me. I see the False Core Beliefs as true— I can't find the truth. It's then that I do my processes or reach out to those I trust to pull me back into the light of healing.

I will not put myself in a position of feeling physically uncomfortable with other people if I have a choice about it. I revere my personal space and honor that of others. That is a physical boundary I hold for myself.

I will not spend time with people who don't treat me with respect. I've spent far too much of my life adjusting, making myself uncomfortable or unhappy so others would feel okay. I'm done accepting unacceptable behavior. That is an emotional boundary I hold for myself.

I don't let my history as a survivor define me as a victim, or that I'm broken and can't be fixed. My False Core Belief that I'm broken will never completely go away, but I will not give it the power to dominate how I feel about myself. That is an internal boundary I hold for myself.

No one can truly know where your boundaries need to be but you. Do not allow the thoughts or fears of others to stray you from your truth. William Shakespeare wrote many powerful words, and for me, none more powerful than this— "To thine own self be true." Take heed of the opinions of others, but you are your own best authority, no one else.

I wish you strength and happiness in your healing journey.

Acknowledgements

Special thanks (in no particular order) go out to Corey Roskin, Dennis Courtney, Terry Ray, Steven Rosenbaum, Adam Karsten, Stan Zimmerman, Marguerite Von Durkheim, Joy Langer, Lesley Moore, Erin Nanasi, Julie Warder, C. Andrew Mayer, Mary Elizabeth Bartlett, Mark Milhone, Meshach Weber, Kia Lee, Jana Goodermont, The SAKI team, Kenosha Davenport, Ashley Taylor Gouge, DStew, Jess Rau, Bob and Susan Mortenson, Kim Mortenson, Lee Adams, Larry LaFond, Tessa Walker, Angela Landis, Melanie Blue, Kudra Wagner, Clare Merritt, Annie Enneking, TJ O'Donnell, Jina Penn-Tracy, Donald Goff, Maria Asp, Eden Alair, Ellen Harvey, Kristen Froebel, Molly McManus, Robb Shapiro, C. Amanda Maud, Stacey Allen, Melissa Beneke, Scott Stearns, Lynn and Sandy Stearns, Jeremy Norton, Rhianon Fiskradatz, Beth Desotelle, Barbara Brooks, Constance Cilva, Robert Dorfman, Robb Krueger, Dayna Steele, Charlie Justiz, Norah Shapiro, Elizabeth Larsen, Jeffrey Hatcher, Medaria Arradondo, Elena Giannetti, Bridget Sullivan, Cordelia Anderson, Ian Leask, Gary Lindberg, Susan Thurston-Hamerski, Dawn McClelland, Michael Shaw, Clark Dugger, and Craig Wells.

I'd like to extend my deepest thanks to the following people, who have been instrumental in my journey, and who have supported me in the development of this book:

Kim Anderson and Tony Griffiths for your love and support and for asking me the right questions to help me see what my future could be. Kam Sisco for being the best pal a gal could want. Rana Haugen, for being a beacon of calm and keeping me true to myself. Wayne Bryan, for your keen eye and exceptional insight in assisting me with the copy editing of this book. Shanan Custer, for your undying support and ability to spot even the most elusive typos. Ellie Hyatt for your unwavering friendship and support. Ricardo Levins Morales, for your guidance and friendship. The Bad Ass Crones, for being the marker for my center. Brad Stearns, for kicking me in the butt when I needed it. Alan Carvalho, Shelley Kaplan, and Doug Schmidt— I would literally not be living the life I live today without you. Thank you. My parents, Jan and Dean Stearns— I miss you.

And finally, Tucker, Calvin, and Tasha Adams for being the best children (and bonus daughter) a mother could want. I love you with all my heart.

About the Author

LAURA STEARNS studied theater as a child actor and has been working in professional theater since the age of thirteen. As a theater-maker in the Twin Cities, which included twelve years on staff at the world-renowned Guthrie Theater, Laura worked with some of the most talented artists from around the world, both on and off stage. Laura is an accomplished actor and director with a diverse skill set that has given her the opportunity to work in almost every department of theater production. Now living in Southern California, she was the recipient of the 2024 Desert Theatre League Award for Best Direction of *The Woman in the Mirror* in Palm Springs. She continues to work in theater as an actor, designer, director, and playwright and is a fierce advocate for safe spaces in theater production and education.

www.ingramcontent.com/pod-product-compliance
Lightning Source LLC
Chambersburg PA
CBHW071745120626
46550CB00002B/668